MICROWAVE COOKING
PROPERLY EXPLAINED

To Huw, Emma and Lindsay
with thanks for their honest opinions
and their continued encouragement.

Cover illustration
Orange-Glazed Gammon (page 92) and Pears in Cider (page 126) cooked in a Whirlpool M914 Crisp Grill Microwave by Caroline Young, and photographed by Paul Noble.

MICROWAVE COOKING
PROPERLY EXPLAINED

WITH RECIPES

Annette Yates

RIGHT WAY

Printed and bound in Great Britain by Cox & Wyman Ltd., Reading, Berkshire.

The *Right Way* series is published by Elliot Right Way Books, Brighton Road, Lower Kingswood, Tadworth, Surrey, KT20 6TD, U.K. For information about our company and the other books we publish, visit our web site at www.right-way.co.uk

CONTENTS

ACKNOWLEDGEMENTS

I could not have written this book without the help and kindness of many people – the Microwave Technologies Association and their members, several microwave manufacturers, makers and suppliers of microwave cookware and my home economics colleagues in the microwave industry – all of whom have generously shared their expertise with me. My thanks go to each and every one.

INTRODUCTION

I welcomed the opportunity to update this book. On reading the original text I soon realised that during the writing of it I had been more than a little guilty of treating the microwave as the ultimate answer to all cooking. Over the years my attitude has matured and I now see the microwave oven not as an isolated appliance but as a valuable part of the kitchen team. Today, my microwave works hand in hand with the hob, the grill, the toaster, the kettle and, sometimes, the conventional oven. No longer am I prepared to cook foods in the microwave oven simply 'because you can'. If I cannot get the best results, I use a better method. As a consequence, many of the old recipes have been replaced by new ones – recipes which have been tried and tested by family and friends and which have cooked successfully in a variety of microwave ovens. You will notice too, that many of the recipes make use of a variety of microwave power levels – to get the best results every time.

One section of the book has been omitted entirely. 'Meal Planning' described the juggling involved in creating an entire three-course meal in the microwave – including soup, a joint of beef, Parsley Baked Onions and Baked Potatoes, with Plum and Walnut Compote to follow. Of course, it can be done, but these days, I rarely try it, unless the meal involves something simple – like a cold dessert, for which I will have melted chocolate or dissolved gelatine in the microwave, and a one-pot main course to be served with salad and bread. I avoid cooking complicated courses with several accompaniments – there is a danger of spending longer in the kitchen than bargained for, and, much as I love cooking, I too seem to have less and less time to divide between my responsibilities.

Instead, I prefer to cook some parts of the meal in the microwave while simultaneously cooking the rest on the hob or under the grill. This is my route to the largest time savings and superior meals.

This book is all about fitting a microwave into your life, not about fitting your life around a microwave. If you have recently acquired your first oven, try not to be too hard on yourself. The best way to gain confidence is to take one step at a time, using the microwave to cook one part of each meal. It will soon earn its keep, once you have had the time to get to know it and the foods it cooks best for *you*. In no time at all, you will wonder how you ever managed without it.

To those of you who are already confident with your microwave oven, I hope you will pick up many handy tips and enjoy the recipes, many of which are new to the book.

Happy microwaving!

Annette Yates

1

ADVANTAGES
AND LIMITATIONS

Before buying a microwave, you need to know how it will benefit you and what it is capable of achieving.

What are the advantages of microwave cooking?
* Cooking times are much shorter. Conventional cooking times can be cut by as much as 60-75%.

* Food can be thawed quickly using a microwave.

* It's economical. A microwave uses about 25% of the power needed to run a conventional oven (a combination oven uses a little more). Added to this, cooking times are shorter and, when you make full use of a microwave, the lower the power level used, the lower the electricity consumption.

* It's versatile. Most foods can be thawed, cooked and reheated in a microwave.

* It's convenient. Snacks and meals can be prepared as and when they are needed. A microwave copes particularly well with small quantities and single portions, and in households where individuals eat at different times, a microwave is a boon.

* It's easy to use. A microwave can be plugged in anywhere there is 13 amp socket. Controls are generally straightforward to use. Oven cleaning is minimal too.

* It saves on washing up, because many foods can be cooked in their serving dishes.

* Microwaves are clean and cool, and are particularly suitable for use by elderly and disabled people and children.

* Low-fat and fat-free cooking is easy with a microwave.

* Flavour and nutritive value are excellent in foods cooked in a microwave. Many foods can be cooked simply in their own juices; others with just a little additional liquid. Cooking foods for the briefest time, and in the least liquid, is known to be one of the best ways to retain maximum food value.

Is there anything a microwave can't do?

* Browning and crisping are not possible unless the microwave oven has a grill or it is a combination oven (see page 19).

* Frying, either in shallow or deep fat, is not possible.

* It cannot successfully cook eggs in their shells.

* A microwave cannot make toast, unless it incorporates an efficient grill.

* It cannot make pancakes.

* A microwave cannot cook crusty pastry and bread, foods in batter, Yorkshire pudding, roast potatoes or soufflés, unless it is a combination oven (see page 19).

* Heating more than 300ml (½ pt) water is more economical in an electric kettle.

* A microwave cannot speed up the cooking of some foods. Rice, pasta and pulses, for example, generally take as long to cook in the microwave as they do conventionally.

To sum up
A microwave oven is invaluable when used, not as an isolated appliance, but as part of the team of cooking equipment in the kitchen. Used together with the hob, grill, kettle, toaster and conventional oven, a microwave oven will help you to get the best results in the shortest time.

2
THE MICROWAVE

What are microwaves and how do they cook food?
Cooking with microwaves is quite different from conventional methods which use electricity, gas or solid fuel. In a conventional oven the walls and the air inside them are heated first. As the oven heats up, so does the surface of the food. This surface heat, in turn, is slowly conducted to the centre of the food.

In a microwave oven the walls and air are not heated. The microwaves pass straight into the food, to heat it directly.

Microwaves are electromagnetic waves, similar to radio and television waves. Electric energy is converted into microwaves by a valve called a magnetron. The microwaves are channelled along a wave guide, then a stirrer or paddle distributes them evenly into the oven cavity. Once they are inside the oven, three things happen to the microwaves.

1. They are *reflected* off the metal walls and bounce around inside the oven cavity.

2. They are *transmitted* by glass, china, pottery, microwave plastics and paper. So the microwaves pass straight through dishes made of these materials.

3. They are *absorbed* by water (in particular) in food. When the water molecules absorb microwave energy they become agitated and vibrate at an incredible speed – about 2,450 million times per second! It is this excitement which generates the heat which, in turn, cooks the food in a very short time. Microwaves can only penetrate food about 4cm (1½ in), so

anything thicker than 8cm (3 in) relies on heat from the outer areas being conducted to the centre – just like conventional cooking.

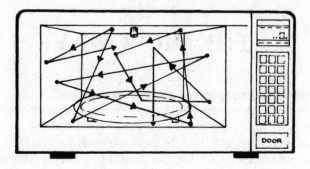

Fig. 1.   The metal walls of the oven reflect the microwaves.
(Food is not shown in the oven for the purposes of this diagram, but remember, a microwave oven should never be switched on empty.)

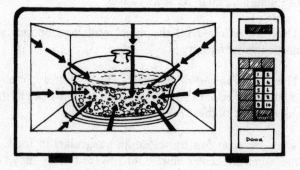

Fig. 2.   Certain cooking containers transmit microwaves.

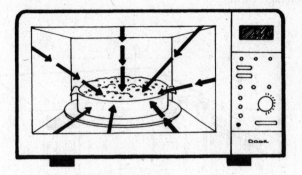

Fig. 3. Food absorbs microwaves and heats up.

Are microwaves safe?

* Microwaves produce a change in temperature only. They should not be confused with X-rays.

* Microwaves cannot be produced unless the oven door is securely closed. The doors and hinges are fitted with locks, seals and cut-out switches which automatically switch off the microwaves the instant the door is opened.

* The mesh in the oven door allows the cook to see inside the oven, but the holes in this mesh are not large enough to allow the microwaves to escape. They simply bounce off the mesh back into the oven cavity.

* British safety standards regarding leakage of microwave ovens are extremely strict. Ovens are built to precise specifications and they are thoroughly tested before leaving the factory. When buying a microwave oven, look for the BEAB (British Electrotechnical Approvals Board) label for household appliances, which means that a microwave oven

has met safety requirements dictated by the relevant British Standard Specification for electrical safety and microwave leakage limits.

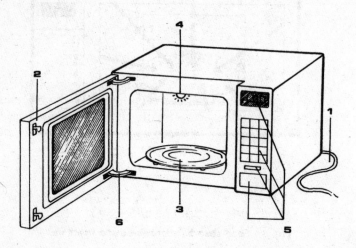

Fig. 4.   The main parts of a microwave oven
1. Lead from oven to 13 amp plug.
2. Door fastening. There may be two or more locking devices to ensure that microwaves are switched off as soon as the door is opened.
3. Removable shelf or turntable. This raises the food off the oven floor, so that microwaves can be absorbed from underneath too. It makes the job of mopping up spilled food easier and it also ensures that the food is in the best position to receive the microwaves (with a turntable, the food is carried around the oven to ensure even absorption of microwaves).
4. Interior light. This usually lights as soon as the oven is switched on.
5. Controls. Basic controls include an on/off button, a timer control and a control to adjust the microwave power level.
6. Door stop.

3

CHOOSING A MICROWAVE OVEN

Choosing a microwave oven is an exciting experience, so long as you are not intimidated by the vast choice on offer today. This section lists some of the questions worth answering before buying. It then goes on to outline many of the features on offer today. Whether you are buying your first microwave or you are updating your current model, I hope to help you choose one which will fit in with the way you cook and eat.

How much do you want to spend?
Though price may dictate your choice initially, deciding which features you would like on an oven will also help to narrow down a price band.

How much space do you have and where?
Will the microwave sit on the kitchen work surface or on a shelf or brackets, or will you want it built into the kitchen? Do you wish to move it around, perhaps on self-catering holidays? Remember it needs to be close to a 13 amp socket. Most ovens need ventilation, so check you will be able to leave a space all round yours. Position the oven so that you have a small area of work surface next to it — for taking dishes out of the microwave and setting them down.

Will your microwaving be restricted to thawing and reheating?
If so, a basic model will be sufficient — a low wattage oven with cooking, heating and defrost settings. If, however, you will want to make full use of the microwave oven and cook all the things it does well — soups, snacks, sauces, fish, vegetables, poultry, casseroles, fruit and puddings — you will

need at least 600W and several power levels (see opposite).

How many do you cook for?

Check the inside of the microwave oven. Is it large enough to take your largest casserole dish, or the largest item you are likely to cook? Will your dishes fit, and turn round, on the turntable? Even if you cook for one or two people most of the time, are you likely to cook for large numbers in the future?

Do you already have an efficient grill?

If not, you may consider buying a microwave oven which incorporates a grill (see page 18).

Do you regularly cook roast meals, pastry, cakes or oven-cooked food coated in breadcrumbs or batter?

If so, you may consider buying a combination oven (see page 19) which combines the heat of a traditional oven with microwave cooking.

FEATURES ON MICROWAVE AND COMBINATION OVENS

Controls can be mechanical or touch-control. Both are easy to use, but for accurate timing in seconds (for softening butter, for instance) choose a digital display. Touch-control panels are easy to wipe clean.

Oven interiors can be stainless steel or plastic-coated. Both are easy to clean, and personal preference will dictate which you choose. Combination ovens (see page 19) often have at least one self-clean lining; some top-of-the-range models have a pyrolytic cleaning function — the oven can be heated to a temperature which is high enough to burn off any food residue.

A *turntable* helps food to cook evenly by raising it off the oven floor so the microwaves can reach underneath, and by turning the food as it cooks. When buying a microwave with a turntable, check that your cooking containers and plates are not so large that they prevent the turntable turning.

Wave stirrers or paddles, also encourage even cooking by distributing the microwaves evenly into the oven cavity. Some ovens have both a turntable and wave stirrers.

Power output indicates the amount of microwave energy used to cook food. It ranges from 500W to 1000W. The higher the wattage (W) the faster the microwave cooks. Recipes in magazines and books (including this one), and cooking times on many pre-packed foods, are generally based on 600-700W. If you buy a more powerful oven, you will need either to reduce the cooking time by about 25%, or to lower the power level to the equivalent of 600-700W and cook for the normal time. If you buy a 500W model you will need to lengthen cooking times by about 30%.

Power levels control the amount of microwave energy entering the oven, so food can be cooked as quickly or as slowly as you like. Manufacturers vary in the way they describe power levels − some have up to nine settings but the most useful are HIGH (100%), MEDIUM-HIGH (75%), MEDIUM (50%), MEDIUM-LOW (30%) and LOW (10%).

A *shelf* allows more food to be cooked at the same time, though cooking times will be longer. The same amount of microwave energy goes into the oven, no matter how much food it holds, and this energy has to be shared out.

An *auto-minute* button is handy. Just press it to cook for 1 minute on HIGH (100%).

Quick/Rapid/Jet start or *Boost* is designed for quick heating of liquids and drinks in particular. It usually works on a higher power than that used for everyday cooking.

A *minute timer* or alarm can sometimes be used as an automatic timer, with no cooking involved.

Auto-defrost is a useful feature, though most foods can be thawed on DEFROST or MEDIUM-LOW (30%). Auto-defrost is controlled either by time or by the weight of the food. Some models have a sensor which weighs the food and automatically calculates the thawing time.

Auto cook/heat allows you to program in the type of food and its weight, then the oven does the rest — calculating the cooking time, appropriate power levels and, in combination ovens, the temperature. Some models have an automatic sensing device which does this. This auto-cook/heat feature is particularly useful for large pieces of meat and for ready meals.

Hold-warm puts the oven on a low power level to keep food warm for 15 minutes or more.

Multi-sequence cooking allows you to program the oven to cook on a series of cooking times and power levels — for example, cooking on HIGH (100%) for a set time, switching to MEDIUM (50%) for a set time, then holding on LOW (10%) for a time.

Auto-repeat recalls the last program used.

A *memory* function stores programs — useful only if you cook the same dishes frequently.

Delay-start/Pre-set/Auto-start delays cooking for several hours if necessary, perhaps while you are out. This feature is more useful in a combination oven (for conventional or combination cooking) than in a microwave where cooking times are very short anyway and food may need turning or stirring.

A *grill* is useful for improving the appearance of microwaved food, and if you do not already have an efficient conventional grill. Don't expect a grill in a microwave oven to be as powerful as a conventional grill, though, and it is likely to operate only with the door closed. Some ovens allow simultaneous grilling and microwaving to save time. Grills with radiant elements are similar to conventional electric grills. Halogen bulbs give instant heat, though they are usually restricted to only one area of the oven ceiling. A quartz grill is both quick and efficient.

A *combination oven* combines the speed of microwaving with the traditional heat of a conventional oven. Foods can be browned and crisped as well as cooked in a fraction of the usual time. A combination oven is particularly useful if you regularly cook whole poultry and meat joints, pastry, cakes, Yorkshire pudding, soufflés and other foods which need a crisp and brown finish.

As the name suggests, a combination oven can be used in three ways: on microwave only, on convection only (using traditional heat in °C), or with a combination of the two (often called 'combination', 'dual-cook' or 'Hi-speed'). It is when cooking on 'combination' that models vary in the way they work. There are three main types:

* where both the temperature and the microwave power level can be controlled by you;

* where the temperature can be controlled, while the microwave power level is pre-set;

* where there are a series of pre-set programs in which specific temperatures are already matched up with selected microwave power levels.

Your choice will depend on whether you are a keen cook who likes to experiment, and who prefers to be able to adjust temperature and microwave power in order to achieve the results you want; or whether you prefer to have it all selected for you, ready simply to press a button.

Rotisserie units feature in some combination ovens, for cooking meat and poultry on a spit, using a combination of microwaving, grilling and convected heat.

An extra word on choice
When making your final choice, it is worth asking to see the instruction books and cook books which accompany the ovens. Some are better than others.

Microwave labels

A voluntary labelling scheme for microwave ovens and food packs was introduced in 1992. It was developed by the Ministry of Agriculture, Fisheries and Food (MAFF) in partnership with oven manufacturers, food manufacturers, retailers and consumer organisations. It is designed to help us to microwave food more successfully, particularly when heating small quantities of food, such as ready meals for one or two.

New microwave ovens are now labelled with:

* the power output of the oven, based on an internationally agreed standard (IEC 705);

* a heating category letter, from A to E, to indicate the oven's ability to heat small food packs.

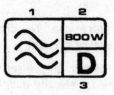

Fig. 5.   The microwave labelling scheme.
1. Microwave symbol.
2. Power output (watts).
3. Heating category for small packs.

The aim is for all small (up to 500g) food packs which are suitable for microwaving to be marked with the microwave symbol plus appropriate heating category letters and cooking times. Then, you simply match up the information on the food pack with that on your microwave oven.

If you bought your microwave oven before the labelling scheme started, and you would like to know its power output under the new scheme, a free booklet 'The New Microwave Labels' is available. It lists models together with their power output and, where possible, their heating categories. For your copy, write to Food Sense, London SE99 7TT.

4

CONTAINERS FOR
THE MICROWAVE

The containers which are suitable for microwave cooking are those which allow microwaves to pass straight through them into the food. You'll probably find that many of the dishes you already own will be fit for use in the microwave. Those which have their own lids are the most convenient.

What to use
Ovenglass, glass ceramic, china and some pottery are suitable. Although they let microwaves pass through them, you will probably still need to use oven gloves to lift them from the microwave oven, because the heat conducted from the food makes the dishes hot. Also, because they absorb a lot of heat from the food, cooking in these containers may take slightly longer than in materials which are specially designed for the microwave.

A wide range of microwave cookware is available today, not only in heat-resistant plastic, but also in ovenglass and ceramic glass. The most versatile are suitable for microwave, conventional oven, freezer and dishwasher. They are usually fit for cooking foods which reach a very high temperature, such as those containing a high proportion of fat or sugar. Always check the labels before buying.

Paper, soft plastics and basketware should only be used for brief heating.

What not to use
Metal containers reflect microwaves and, in general, should

not be used when microwaving.

Some microwave manufacturers suggest using small pieces of foil to shield food and prevent it overcooking − follow the instructions carefully. Others suggest cooking some foods in foil trays − do check with the instruction book and follow the method carefully. If the manufacturer of your oven does not advise it, don't do it − if anything were to go wrong, your guarantee would be affected.

Do not use plates or dishes which are decorated with gold, silver or metal paint. The microwaves will cause the metal to spark and blacken.

Avoid using unglazed or partly-glazed pottery, fine glass (it contains minute particles of metal), polystyrene, dairy product containers, and dishes which have been repaired with glue.

To test if a container is suitable for the microwave
Put the dish in the microwave oven and place a cup containing 150ml (¼ pt) cold water inside it. Cook on HIGH (100%) for 1-2 minutes. The outer dish should remain cool while the water in the cup heats up. If the dish becomes warm, it has absorbed some of the microwaves and is unsuitable for use.

The shape matters
Circular containers are best because the microwaves reach the food equally from all sides. Though the centre usually cooks more slowly than the edges, stirring food during cooking encourages even results.

A *ring* shape produces best results and is particularly useful for foods which cannot be stirred − like cakes. There is no slow-cooking centre, so the food cooks evenly.

Squares and rectangles tend to overcook at their corners, where the microwaves are concentrated. They often have an area in the centre which cooks only slowly.

Straight sides on a container help the food to cook evenly. Sloping sides allow microwaves to concentrate in, and overcook, food at the outer edge.

Food wraps
Roasting bags and *microwave bags* are useful for microwave

cooking. Follow the packet instructions for use. Ordinary polythene food bags are not suitable.

Cling film can be used to cover dishes but do not allow it to touch the food. Pierce it, or turn back a small area, to allow steam to escape during cooking.

Absorbent kitchen paper, greaseproof paper and *non-stick baking paper* are useful for wrapping or covering foods.

Useful accessories

A *microwave rack* is handy to encourage even cooking of all foods − to raise dishes in the oven so that the microwaves can easily reach the food from every direction. They are also useful for thawing meat and other foods, preventing them from sitting in a pool of liquid.

Browning dishes are useful in microwave-only ovens. They have a special coating which heats up in the microwave, for searing and browning small items such as bacon, sausages, steaks, chops, eggs, fish, vegetables and toasted sandwiches. The surface of a browning dish can reach a temperature of up to 300°C (600°F). Always use oven gloves, follow the dish manufacturer's instructions carefully and never exceed the recommended pre-heating time. Once the food is put on to the hot surface, cooking is completed by microwaving.

A *plate ring* is useful for stacking plated meals for thawing or reheating in the microwave. Best results are obtained if no more than two plates are stacked.

5

USING THE MICROWAVE

A microwave oven is a versatile piece of equipment which thaws, cooks and reheats food at a moment's notice. As you get to know your oven, you will discover that several things affect thawing/cooking/reheating times and the way the microwave performs generally:

* the type of food, its moisture content (the more it contains, the longer it takes to cook) and its density (dense foods like meat take longer to thaw than porous foods such as bread and cake);

* the quantity of food − two potatoes take longer to cook than one, though not necessarily double the time − for this reason, avoid filling the microwave with food;

* its shape and size − regular shapes cook more evenly than irregular shapes, and small pieces cook quicker than large pieces;

* the starting temperature of the food dictates how long it takes to thaw/cook/reheat − for instance, food from the refrigerator takes longer to cook than food at room temperature;

* the container used − and its shape in particular − a circular shape with straight sides is best (see page 22);

* the power level used − the higher the power level the faster the cooking;

* the way in which a food is cooked conventionally − food which normally requires slow, gentle cooking will benefit from cooking on a low power level in the microwave;

* the arrangement of the food – even layers encourage even heating; arrange individual foods in a circle with thicker areas towards the edge of the dish;

* turning, stirring and repositioning foods encourages even results too;

* the standing time – most foods should be allowed to stand for a short time after microwaving – to allow the temperature to even out and to allow the food to finish thawing, cooking or reheating.

THAWING FOOD

A microwave and a freezer make a good partnership. Food which normally takes hours to thaw out can be taken from the freezer and thawed in the microwave in a matter of minutes.

Food is thawed using the DEFROST or MEDIUM-LOW (30%) setting. The food is subjected to microwave energy in short bursts for about 30% of the time period (in some ovens it is possible to hear the energy switching on and off as it pulsates into the oven). By controlling the microwave energy in this way, the food thaws slowly and evenly – during the periods when no microwaves are entering the oven, heat from the thawed areas is conducted to the colder areas. If the microwaves were not controlled, the food would thaw too quickly around the edges, heating up while the centre remained frozen solid.

After thawing, food should be allowed to stand for a short period, to allow any remaining ice crystals to disappear and to allow the temperature of the food to even out.

Many microwave ovens have an AUTO-DEFROST setting, which thaws food even more gently and incorporates a standing time too. Some models are controlled by time, during which the oven (which starts thawing on a fairly high power) gradually reduces the power level to LOW (10%). Some are controlled by the weight of the food – you simply programme the oven with the type and weight of food to be thawed, and the oven does the rest. Others have a sensor which weighs the food and automatically calculates the thawing time.

Tips for thawing

* Frozen vegetables need no thawing — they can be cooked straight from the freezer.

* Containers which can be taken from freezer to microwave are the most convenient to use.

* Freeze food in shallow blocks — for quick and even thawing.

* Put a block of frozen food into a close-fitting dish for thawing — to prevent thawed areas spreading over the base of the dish and heating up too soon.

* Before thawing, remove any excess ice which may be attached to food.

* Remove any metal ties, foil or foil containers before thawing.

* Open containers and bags of food before thawing — to prevent them splitting as the air inside heats and expands during thawing.

* Cover most food during thawing — to encourage even thawing in the minimum time. Baked foods, such as cakes, bread and pastries are best left uncovered — to prevent their surfaces from becoming too moist.

* Put cakes, bread and pastries on a sheet of absorbent kitchen paper — to soak up excess moisture during thawing.

* Arrange individual items in a circle, with the centre free, for even results.

* Follow the thawing times given in your oven manufacturer's instruction book until you are familiar with your oven.

* Turn and reposition large or dense foods at least once during thawing.

* Separate foods as they thaw (such as sausages, chops and fish fillets) to encourage even thawing. Break up blocks of food (such as sauces and soups) as they soften.

* Should any part of the food begin to feel warm, stop thawing and allow it to stand for several minutes before starting again.

* Ensure poultry and meat are completely thawed before cooking.

REHEATING FOOD

Food reheats efficiently in a microwave, in a fraction of the time taken conventionally; and its colour, texture and flavour can be just as good as freshly-cooked food.

Tips for reheating

* The colder the food the longer it will take to heat — food from the refrigerator takes longer than food at room temperature.

* Avoid reheating large, solid items, such as a joint of meat. Results are more successful if it is sliced first.

* Arrange food with care — in shallow, even layers. A plate of food should be arranged so that there is one even layer, with thick, dense items towards the edge.

* Two plated meals can be reheated by stacking one on top of the other, with a plate ring between them. Turn the plates (in opposite directions) at least once during reheating.

* Cover or wrap food during reheating — to retain heat and moisture so that it heats evenly and quickly. Bread, pastry, crumble toppings and similar foods which need to be kept dry, should be reheated uncovered.

* Most foods can be reheated on HIGH (100%). Some are better on MEDIUM (50%) or MEDIUM-LOW (30%) — such as bread; large casseroles and dishes like lasagne, moussaka and shepherd's pie; Christmas pudding; fruit; and mince pies.

* Stir foods whenever possible during reheating — such as soups, sauces, casseroles, milk puddings and drinks (see page 149). Turn or reposition large items at least once — such as poultry or meat pieces, whole potatoes, lasagne, moussaka and shepherd's pie.

* Always under-estimate reheating times to avoid overheating food. It is preferable to put the food back in the oven to heat for a little longer, rather than spoil it.

* Make sure that reheated food is *piping hot throughout*.

* Use a food thermometer if you want to make sure that the centre of the food is hot.

* Allow food to stand after reheating − to allow its temperature to even out.

* Some foods improve with reheating − casseroles in particular.

* Pastry and crunchy toppings can lose their crispness if overheated, so heat them carefully.

* Take care when heating pastry with a filling. Although the pastry may feel only warm to touch, the filling is usually much hotter.

CARE OF YOUR MICROWAVE

Look after your oven and follow the manufacturer's instructions and it will reward you with years of reliable service. Avoid operating the oven while it is empty − make sure by keeping a small container of water in the oven in case someone switches it on in error. Do not use metal containers in the oven (unless the manufacturer allows this), do not allow anything to jam in the door (tea towels, for instance) and never lean heavily on the door. Lastly, make sure that every member of the household knows how to operate the oven correctly.

Keeping a microwave oven clean is usually a simple matter of wiping out the oven after each use. The walls of the oven don't heat up during cooking, so food does not bake on them as it does in a conventional oven. This is not the case with a combination oven, however, which does heat up and, because the cavity is smaller than a conventional oven and the oven walls are closer to the cooking food, splashes can easily burn on.

Tips for cleaning microwave and combination ovens

* Wipe out the interior frequently and regularly.

* Mop up spills and splashes as soon as they occur − spilled food and splashes will only slow down the cooking the next time the oven is used.

* Removable parts, such as a turntable or a shelf, should be washed with hot water and detergent, then thoroughly dried.

* For heavy soiling, put a bowl of water in the microwave oven and cook on HIGH (100%) until it boils — the steam produced will help to soften stubborn marks, which can then be wiped away with a soft cloth.

* To remove lingering odours from the oven, add some lemon juice to the water.

* Do not use abrasive cleaners on any part of a microwave or combination oven, and never use a knife to clean off a stubborn mark.

* Never allow water or cleaning materials to enter any vents in the oven cavity.

* To clean stubborn stains from a combination oven, use liquid cleaners only.

* Look for specially-designed microwave oven cleaners too.

Replacement parts
In the event that an oven part needs replacing (such as a turntable, shelf or bulb), obtain it from an authorised service agent. To find out your nearest one, contact the manufacturer of your oven (the address and telephone number should be in your instruction book).

If a fault occurs
Always obtain qualified help — from an authorised service engineer. Never remove the outer casing of the oven or attempt to repair a fault yourself.

Servicing
If you use your oven correctly and do not move it around frequently or drop it, there's little need to have it checked. However, if you have reason to believe that the oven has been damaged in any way, or if you notice a change in its

performance, you may wish to have it checked by an authorised engineer.

Many manufacturers offer a service contract on new ovens.

Leakage testing

If you look after your oven, there is little need to have it checked (see page 29). A microwave oven which has been damaged sufficiently (by dropping it, for instance) to allow leakage, will not work. However, over the years many people have spoken to me, simply *wondering* whether their oven leaks. My answer is always reassuring, but I also understand that once doubts are instilled in the mind, mistrust lingers. In these instances, I suggest that it is worth putting their mind at ease by having the oven checked over by a qualified engineer.

Over recent years consumers have been tempted to buy low-cost hand-held leakage testers. They have all proved to be unreliable. At the time of publication, there is still nothing as dependable as those used by authorised engineers and environmental health officers. Their testers are substantial and costly machines which are recalibrated regularly to make sure they are accurate.

6

ABOUT THE RECIPES

* Ingredients are given in metric and imperial. Follow one type of measure for successful results.

* All spoon quantities are level unless otherwise stated.

* The recipes in this book have been tested in 600-700W microwave ovens. If your oven has a higher wattage, you can either cook on HIGH (100%) and reduce the cooking times slightly (by about 25%) or use a lower power level which is the equivalent of 600-700W and cook for the recommended time. If your oven is less than 600W, you will need to increase the cooking times by about 30%.

* When a food should be covered (or uncovered) during cooking, the method states this. If no instruction is given, then it makes little difference whether you cover the food or not.

* All cooking is on HIGH (100%) unless otherwise stated.

* In ovens without turntables, food may need turning or repositioning occasionally.

* Each recipe starts with the number of servings, an approximate cooking time and a note indicating whether it is suitable for freezing.

* When a recipe benefits from using a grill, this is also indicated at the start of the recipe.

Combination ovens
There are no recipes for combination cooking (that is, using conventional oven heat together with microwaves) in this book. Instead, my colleague Caroline Young and I have created over 100 recipes for combination ovens and microwave ovens with built-in grills for *The Combination Microwave Cook*, also published by Elliot Right Way Books.

7

SOUPS AND STARTERS

Home-made soups are quick and easy in a microwave, whether you are making an individual portion or enough for a family.

Those of us who still like to make the occasional pot of good home-made stock find it convenient to put the broken-up bones, chicken carcass or well-washed vegetable peelings into a bowl, cover them with water and cook for about 30 minutes (or more, if you prefer). When the mixture is strained, you have a delicious fresh stock ready for adding to sauces and, in particular, to soups.

Tips for cooking soups
* Use a large, deep bowl so that the soup has plenty of room to boil up. This is particularly important when a recipe contains milk.

* When cooking a conventional soup recipe in the microwave, reduce the quantity of liquid by about one quarter. There is

usually less evaporation in the microwave. If the finished soup is too thick, it can always be diluted after cooking.

* Cut ingredients such as vegetables into even pieces to encourage even cooking. The smaller they are cut, the quicker they will cook.

* The cooking time can be speeded up by adding *boiling* water or stock to the main ingredients (a kettle boils a large quantity of water far more efficiently than a microwave). To speed up cooking even further, use half the liquid only, then add the extra (hot) after cooking.

* Cover soup to keep the moisture and heat in. A lid with a vent helps to prevent it boiling over. If you don't have a vented lid, put a wooden cocktail stick between the bowl and lid.

* Stir the soup occasionally to encourage even cooking.

* Most soups can be cooked on HIGH (100%). Remember, the cooking time will depend on the ingredient with the longest cooking time.

* If a soup contains meat which requires tenderising, rice, pasta or other cereals, it will cook just as quickly if it is first brought to the boil on HIGH (100%), then cooked on MEDIUM (50%) or MEDIUM-LOW (30%) for the remaining time. In the same way, a soup can be left to simmer gently for as long as you wish, to develop its flavour, just as you would leave it on the hob.

* *Dried soups:* Make up the soup mix with hot water (from the kettle) following the packet instructions. Cook on HIGH (100%) stirring occasionally, until the soup boils. Lower the microwave power to MEDIUM (50%) or MEDIUM-LOW (30%), cover and cook for the time stated on the packet, stirring occasionally.

* *Cans and cartons of soups:* Pour the soup into a bowl, diluting it according to label instructions if necessary. Cover and cook on HIGH (100%), stirring occasionally, until hot.

FRESH TOMATO SOUP

Cooking: 25 mins on HIGH *(100%)*

Serves 4-6
Will freeze

25g (1 oz) butter
1 bacon rasher, rind removed and finely chopped
1 medium onion, finely chopped
1 carrot, finely chopped
10ml (2 tsp) sugar
450g (1 lb) fresh tomatoes, chopped; or
   400g can chopped tomatoes
450ml (¾ pt) boiling chicken stock
salt and pepper
bouquet garni
10ml (2 tsp) lemon juice
30ml (2 tbsp) tomato purée
chopped parsley to serve
croûtons or crusty bread, to serve

1. Put the butter, bacon, onion, carrot and sugar in a large bowl. Cover and cook for 5 mins.

2. Add the remaining ingredients. Cover and cook for 20 mins, stirring occasionally.

3. Allow the soup to stand for 10 mins then remove the bouquet garni.

4. Purée the soup in a blender or food processor. (For a really smooth soup, strain through a sieve after puréeing.)

5. Reheat if necessary. Sprinkle with chopped parsley and serve with croûtons or crusty bread.

CREAM OF TOMATO SOUP

Follow method for FRESH TOMATO SOUP and stir in 150ml (¼ pt) single or double cream before serving.

FRENCH ONION SOUP   *Serves 4-6*
Cooking: soup 25 mins on HIGH *(100%)*
          bread 1-2 mins on HIGH *(100%) or under grill*
Will freeze without the bread and cheese

40g (1½ oz) butter
450g (1 lb) onions, finely sliced
600ml (1 pt) boiling beef stock
15ml (1 tbsp) Worcestershire sauce
salt and pepper
4 slices of French bread
75g (3 oz) Cheddar or Gruyère cheese, grated

1. Put the butter and onions in a large bowl, cover and cook for 5 mins.

2. Add the boiling stock, Worcestershire sauce and seasoning. Cover and cook for 15-20 mins, stirring occasionally.

3. Arrange the bread slices on a plate and top with the cheese. Cook, uncovered, for 1-2 mins until the cheese has melted. Float them on top of the soup, to serve.

OR

Pour the soup into a flameproof casserole dish, float the bread slices on top, sprinkle with cheese and cook under a hot grill until the cheese bubbles.

CREAM OF ONION SOUP
Follow stages 1-2 for FRENCH ONION SOUP, then purée in a blender or food processor and stir in 150ml (¼ pt) single cream. Omit the bread and cheese. Instead, fry some onion rings in butter until crisp and brown and scatter over the soup to serve.

CREAMY BUTTER BEAN AND BACON SOUP

Cooking: 20 mins on HIGH *(100%)*   *Serves 4-6*
Will freeze without the cream and parsley

25g (1 oz) butter
1 medium onion, finely chopped
4 lean rashers bacon, rinds removed and finely chopped
two 439g cans butter beans, drained
600ml (1 pt) boiling chicken stock
2.5ml (½ tsp) dried mixed herbs
salt and pepper
150ml (¼ pt) single cream
chopped parsley, to serve

1. Put the butter, onion and bacon into a large bowl, cover and cook for 5 mins, stirring once.

2. Add the beans, boiling stock, herbs and seasoning. Cover and cook for about 15 mins, stirring occasionally.

3. Using a slotted spoon, lift out one or two spoonfuls of bean mixture and reserve. Purée the remaining soup in a blender or food processor and add the cream.

4. Return the soup to its bowl and add the reserved bean mixture. Reheat for 2-3 mins if necessary, without boiling, then sprinkle with parsley to serve.

LEEK AND POTATO SOUP
Cooking: 20 mins on HIGH (100%)

Serves 4-6
Will freeze

25g (1 oz) butter
2 medium leeks, sliced
1 medium onion, finely chopped
350g (12 oz) potatoes, finely sliced
600ml (1 pt) boiling chicken or vegetable stock
salt and pepper
150ml (¼ pt) double cream
chopped chives, to serve

1. Put the butter, leeks and onion in a large bowl, cover and cook for 5 mins, stirring once.

2. Add the potatoes, boiling stock and seasoning. Cover and cook for 10-15 mins, stirring occasionally, until the vegetables are tender.

3. Purée the soup in a blender or food processor. Stir in the cream.

4. Reheat for 2-3 mins, without boiling, and serve sprinkled with chives.

CHICKEN AND VEGETABLE SOUP

Cooking: 35 mins on HIGH *(100%)*

Serves 4

Will freeze

175-225g (6-8 oz) chicken portion
1 bay leaf
1 garlic clove
bouquet garni
1 small onion, finely chopped
1 medium carrot, diced
1 medium leek, finely sliced
1 celery stick, finely sliced
30ml (2 tbsp) Worcestershire sauce
salt and pepper

1. Put the chicken in a medium bowl with 300ml (½ pt) water, the bay leaf, garlic and bouquet garni. Cover and cook for 20 mins. Allow to stand for 5 mins.

2. Meanwhile, put the onion, carrot, leek and celery into a large bowl, cover and cook for 5 mins, stirring once or twice.

3. Lift the chicken out of its stock, discard the skin and bones and chop the chicken meat into small pieces. Strain the stock, discarding the bay leaf, garlic and bouquet garni.

4. Add the chicken to the vegetables and pour the chicken stock over. Add the Worcestershire sauce, 150ml (¼ pt) water and salt and pepper to taste.

5. Cover and cook for 10-15 mins, stirring occasionally, until the vegetables are tender.

MINTED PEA SOUP   *Serves 4*
Cooking: 15 mins on HIGH *(100%)*   *Will freeze*

1 bunch spring onions
100g (4 oz) frozen peas
100g (4 oz) potatoes, diced
300ml (½ pt) vegetable stock
5ml (1 tsp) concentrated mint sauce
300ml (½ pt) milk
salt and pepper
150ml (¼ pt) double cream

1. Chop the spring onions, reserving some of the green tops for a garnish.

2. Put the onions, peas, potatoes and stock into a large bowl. Cover and cook for 10-15 mins, stirring once, until the vegetables are soft.

3. Allow to stand for 5 mins, then purée the soup in a blender or food processor. Stir in the mint sauce, milk and seasoning to taste.

4. Serve immediately or allow to cool, refrigerate, and serve chilled. Top each bowl of soup with a generous swirl of cream and scatter over the reserved spring onion tops.

HADDOCK AND CORN CHOWDER   *Serves 4*

Cooking: 25 mins on HIGH (100%)   Not suitable for freezing

450g (1 lb) smoked haddock
300ml (½ pt) vegetable stock
1 medium onion, finely chopped
15g (½ oz) butter
450g (1 lb) potatoes, diced
salt and pepper
198g can sweetcorn
300ml (½ pt) milk

1. Put the haddock in a shallow dish and add the stock. Cover and cook for 5 mins. Allow to stand for 10 mins.

2. Meanwhile, put the onion and butter in a large bowl, cover and cook for 3 mins.

3. Lift the haddock from its dish, reserving the stock. Skin and flake the fish, discarding any bones.

4. Add the potatoes and reserved fish stock to the onion. Cover and cook for 10-12 mins, stirring once, until the potatoes are tender. Season to taste.

5. Add the haddock, the sweetcorn with its liquid and the milk. Reheat for 3-5 mins before serving. Do not boil.

CHICKEN LIVER PÂTÉ
Cooking: 11 mins on HIGH *(100%)*

Serves 4-6
Will freeze

25g (1 oz) butter
1 medium onion, finely chopped
1 large garlic clove, crushed
450g (1 lb) chicken livers
2 bay leaves
100g (4 oz) curd cheese
60ml (4 tbsp) Greek yoghurt
30ml (2 tbsp) dry sherry
few drops of hot pepper sauce
parsley sprigs to garnish
crusty bread, toast or biscuits to serve

1. Put the butter, onion and garlic in a medium bowl, cover and cook for 3 mins.

2. Stir in the livers and bay leaves. Cook uncovered for 6-8 mins, stirring occasionally, until the livers are cooked.

3. Allow to cool. Remove and discard the bay leaves.

4. Tip the liver mixture into a blender or food processor. Add the cheese, yoghurt, sherry and pepper sauce and purée until smooth. Put into a serving dish, cover and refrigerate.

5. Garnish with parsley and serve with bread, toast or biscuits.

MUSHROOMS WITH GARLIC

Serves 4

Cooking: 5 mins on HIGH (100%)   *Will freeze*

25g (1 oz) butter
1 garlic clove, crushed
225g (8 oz) small button mushrooms
salt and freshly ground black pepper
15ml (1 tbsp) white wine vinegar
30ml (2 tbsp) chopped parsley
toast triangles to serve

1. Put the butter and garlic in a bowl and cook for ½-1 min until the butter has melted.

2. Stir in the mushrooms, coating them with the butter. Season lightly with salt and pepper and add the vinegar. Cover and cook for 3-4 mins, stirring once or twice.

3. Stir in the parsley and serve with toast.

HOT COURGETTE AND TOMATO SALAD

Cooking: 5-6 mins on HIGH (100%)   *Serves 2*
Not suitable for freezing

1 garlic clove
25g (1 oz) fresh breadcrumbs
2 small courgettes
2 medium tomatoes, sliced
30ml (2 tbsp) French salad dressing

1. Halve the garlic clove and rub the cut sides around the inside of a small ovenproof dish. Add the breadcrumbs and cook for 1-2 mins, stirring frequently, until crisp and golden brown. Allow to stand.

2. Use a potato peeler to cut the courgettes into long ribbons. Arrange them on two small plates with the tomatoes. Sprinkle the dressing over them.

3. Cover and cook each plate for 2 mins (or both plates for about 3 mins), turning them half way through cooking.

4. Top with the crisp crumbs and serve immediately.

SMOKED HAM AND EGG RAMEKINS   *Serves 2*
Cooking: 2 mins on MEDIUM *(50%) Not suitable for freezing*

1 slice smoked ham
2 eggs (make sure they are at room temperature)
salt and freshly ground black pepper
30ml (2 tbsp) Greek yoghurt
paprika

1. Halve the ham and place each piece in a ramekin dish. Break an egg into each and prick the yolks. Add a little seasoning and spoon the yoghurt over.

2. Cook, uncovered, on MEDIUM (50%) for 2 mins or until the eggs are nearly set. Allow to stand for 1-2 mins.

3. Sprinkle with paprika and serve immediately.

HOT GRAPEFRUIT WITH VERMOUTH   *Serves 2*
Cooking: 2½ mins on HIGH *(100%)*   *Not suitable for freezing*

1 grapefruit
10-20ml (2-4 tsp) sweet red vermouth
25g (1 oz) butter
30ml (2 tbsp) soft brown sugar
glacé cherries or orange slices to garnish

1. Halve the grapefruit and put into dishes. Use a grapefruit knife or small sharp knife to cut around and loosen each segment. Pour the vermouth over.

2. In a small bowl, melt the butter for 30 secs and brush over the grapefruit. Sprinkle with the sugar.

3. Cook both dishes together, uncovered, for about 2 mins until hot through.

4. Garnish with glacé cherries or orange slices and serve immediately.

TUNA AND TOMATO PASTA   *Serves 4*
Cooking: 23 mins on HIGH *(100%)*
Will freeze − put the sauce and pasta in separate containers

1 medium onion, finely chopped
2 garlic cloves, crushed
400g can chopped tomatoes
150ml (¼ pt) dry white vermouth
1 vegetable stock cube
175g (6 oz) pasta shapes, such as twists or shells
198g can tuna in brine or oil, drained and flaked
30ml (2 tbsp) chopped fresh herbs, such as basil,
   oregano or fennel

1. Put the onion and garlic into a medium bowl, cover and
   cook for 3 mins.

2. Stir in the tomatoes, vermouth and crumbled stock cube.
   Cover and cook for 10 mins, stirring occasionally.

3. Put the pasta in a large bowl and cover well with boiling
   water. Cook, uncovered, for 7 mins, stirring once or twice.
   Allow to stand for 5 mins.

4. Meanwhile, add the tuna and herbs to the tomato sauce,
   cover and cook for 2-3 mins until hot.

5. Drain the pasta well and serve it topped with the sauce.

SPINACH SALAD WITH HOT BACON DRESSING

Cooking: 5 mins on HIGH *(100%)*   *Serves 4*
Not suitable for freezing

225g (8 oz) fresh young spinach leaves
225g (8 oz) bacon rashers, rinds removed and chopped
30ml (2 tbsp) oil
4 spring onions, finely chopped
15ml (1 tbsp) white wine or cider vinegar
5ml (1 tsp) soft brown sugar
15ml (1 tbsp) whole grain mustard
salt and freshly ground black pepper

1. Wash, trim and dry the spinach, shredding any large leaves. Arrange them in a serving bowl.

2. Put the bacon in a medium bowl and cook, uncovered, for about 5 mins, stirring occasionally, until it begins to brown and crisp. Add the remaining ingredients and cook for 1 min.

3. Pour the bacon dressing over the spinach and serve immediately.

LEMON SOLE WITH SMOKED SALMON
Cooking: 5 mins on HIGH (100%)   *Serves 2*
Not suitable for freezing

2 lemon sole fillets
50g (2 oz) smoked salmon slices
30ml (2 tbsp) dry white vermouth
45ml (3 tbsp) double cream
5ml (1 tsp) cornflour
2 spring onions, finely chopped
squeeze of lemon or lime juice
15ml (1 tbsp) finely chopped parsley

1. Cut each sole fillet in half lengthways. Put a strip of smoked salmon on the skin side of each piece of sole. Roll each from its widest end and secure with a wooden cocktail stick.

2. Arrange the fish, spiral ends up, around the edge of a small shallow dish and add the vermouth. Cover and cook for about 2 mins until the fish is just cooked.

3. Carefully pour the liquid from around the fish into a jug. Whisk in the cream and cornflour, then add the onions. Cook for 2-3 mins, stirring frequently, until the sauce thickens and boils. Stir in the lemon or lime juice and parsley.

4. Serve the fish with the sauce.

STUFFED MUSHROOMS
Cooking: 4 mins on HIGH (100%)

Serves 4
Not suitable for freezing

40g (1½ oz) butter
50g (2 oz) fresh breadcrumbs
50g (2 oz) garlic sausage, finely chopped
50g (2 oz) Cheddar cheese, finely grated
15ml (1 tbsp) chopped parsley
5ml (1 tsp) pesto
beaten egg
salt and freshly ground black pepper
4 large flat mushrooms
parsley sprigs to garnish

1. Put 15g (½ oz) butter in a medium bowl and cook for 30 secs until melted. Stir in the breadcrumbs, sausage, cheese, parsley and pesto. Add sufficient beaten egg to bind the mixture. Season to taste.

2. Remove the stalks from the mushrooms, chop finely and add to the stuffing mixture. Pile the stuffing into the mushrooms and dot with the remaining butter.

3. Cover and cook for 3-4 mins. Garnish with parsley to serve.

MARINATED PRAWN KEBABS – see page 58.

8

FISH

Fish is made for the microwave! It cooks quickly, keeps its shape beautifully and retains all its juices. Cook it whole or in fillets; just as it is, brushed with butter, or in a sauce. No matter which method you choose, so long as you don't overcook it, the texture and taste are wonderful.

Tips for thawing fish

* Thaw fish on DEFROST or MEDIUM-LOW (30%).

* Cover it to ensure even thawing.

* Separate pieces and reposition them as they begin to thaw.

* Take care not to overheat or the fish will start to cook around the edges. If any areas start to feel warm, stop thawing and allow the fish to stand for 5-10 mins before continuing.

Guide to thawing times	
	on DEFROST or MEDIUM-LOW (30%):
Whole round fish	4-6 mins per 450g (1 lb)
Whole flat fish	3-4 mins per 450g (1 lb)
Cutlets, steaks and fillets	3-4 mins per 450g (1 lb)
Prawns and shrimps	2-3 mins per 100g (4 oz)
	3-4 mins per 225g (8 oz)
Scallops	3-4 mins per 225g (8 oz)

Tips for cooking fish

* Make a few slits in the skin of whole fish. This allows steam to escape and prevents the skin from bursting open.

* Use a shallow dish, unless you are cooking fish in a sauce, casserole or soup.

* Arrange fish in an even layer to encourage it to cook evenly. When cooking whole fish, overlap their tails, or lay them side by side with head to tail. With fillets, either roll them up and secure each with a wooden cocktail stick, or tuck the thin ends underneath the thick ends to achieve an even layer. When cooking fish steaks, arrange them with the thinner ends towards the centre of the dish.

* Season with salt after cooking to prevent the fish drying out and the surface from toughening.

* When cooking with butter, best results are achieved if it is melted first and brushed over the fish.

* Cover during cooking, to keep the moisture in.

* Turn whole fish once during cooking.

* Take care not to overcook fish. Shellfish cooks especially quickly and is easily overcooked — for this reason add it to a dish towards the end of cooking.

* Should you find that fish easily overcooks on HIGH (100%), try using a lower power level and cooking for slightly longer.

* Check that fish is cooked by lifting up the flakes with a fork. If it is still slightly undercooked, just lay the flakes back down again and allow the fish to stand and the temperature to even out — the flakes should turn opaque and cook to perfection.

* Allow cooked fish to stand for 3-5 mins before serving.

* *Boil-in-the-bag* fish can be cooked in its bag. Remember to pierce the bag before cooking.

* *Fish in breadcrumbs or batter* is generally not suitable for microwave cooking, though fish fingers are acceptable when cooked on a browning dish (follow the dish manufacturer's instructions).

Guide to cooking times	
	Per 450g (1 lb) on HIGH (100%):
Whole round fish	4 mins
Whole flat fish	3 mins
Steak, cutlets and thick fillets	4-6 mins
Thin fillets	2-3 mins
Prawns, raw	2-4 mins
Scallops, shelled	2-3 mins, adding corals for final 1-2 mins
If you find that fish cooked on HIGH (100%) tends to spit and overcook, try reducing the power to MEDIUM (50%) and cooking for a little longer.	

FISH – Basic method

1. Put the fish in an even layer in a shallow dish. If wished, brush with melted butter, or add 30ml (2 tbsp) water, stock, milk or wine.

2. Cover and cook, using the times opposite as a guide.

3. Allow to stand for 3-5 mins before serving.

MUSSELS – Basic method

1. Put 450-900g (1-2 lb) cleaned mussels in a large bowl. Add 150ml (¼ pt) stock, wine or water and a little finely chopped onion and garlic.

2. Cover and cook for 3-5 mins, shaking the bowl occasionally and removing mussels from the top as they cook. Discard any that refuse to open. Use a slotted spoon to lift the mussels on to a warm dish.

3. Season the sauce with salt and pepper, add some chopped fresh herbs and, if wished, stir in 45ml (3 tbsp) double cream before pouring over the mussels and serving.

PLAICE WITH LEMON SAUCE
Serves 2
Cooking: 6 mins on HIGH *(100%)*   *Not suitable for freezing*

15g (½ oz) butter
4 plaice fillets, skinned
30ml (2 tbsp) chopped parsley
10ml (2 tsp) cornflour
grated rind and juice of half a lemon
45ml (3 tbsp) white wine
2.5ml (½ tsp) sugar
salt and pepper

1. Heat the butter for 30 secs until melted. Brush over the skinned side of each plaice fillet. Sprinkle the parsley over. Roll up the fillets from the thick end and arrange them in a shallow dish.

2. Cover and cook for 4 mins. Allow to stand for 3 mins.

3. Meanwhile, put the cornflour into a bowl or jug and whisk in the remaining ingredients.

4. Cook, uncovered, for 1-2 mins, stirring occasionally, until the sauce thickens and boils.

5. Pour the sauce over the fish and reheat for ½-1 min. Serve immediately.

PLAICE WITH ORANGE SAUCE
Follow the method for PLAICE WITH LEMON SAUCE, using orange rind and juice instead of lemon rind and juice.

TROUT WITH ALMONDS
Cooking: 6 mins on HIGH (100%)

Serves 2
Not suitable for freezing

**2 trout, each weighing about 225g (8 oz), cleaned and
  heads removed**
salt and pepper
25g (1 oz) butter
25g (1 oz) flaked almonds
lemon wedges to serve

1. Using a sharp knife, make one or two shallow slits in the skin
   on each side of the trout. Season inside with salt and pepper.

2. Heat half the butter for 30 secs until melted. Brush the trout
   with butter, then arrange them, head to tail, in a shallow dish.

3. Cover and cook for about 4 mins or until just cooked, gently
   turning the fish over half way through cooking. Keep warm.

4. Meanwhile, put the remaining butter in a heatproof dish and
   heat for 30 secs until melted. Stir in the almonds and cook for
   2-3 mins, stirring frequently, until golden brown.

5. Pour the almonds and butter over the trout and serve
   immediately with lemon wedges.

FISH IN PAPER PARCELS   *Serves 4*
Cooking: 10 mins on HIGH (100%)   *Not suitable for freezing*

4 baby carrots, cut into thin matchsticks
4 spring onions, finely sliced
50g (2 oz) mushrooms, finely sliced
oil
4 fish steaks or fillets, such as cod, salmon or halibut,
  each weighing about 175g (6 oz)
30ml (2 tbsp) chopped fresh herbs, such as dill, fennel or
  parsley
50g (2 oz) butter

1. Put the carrots, onions and mushrooms in a small bowl, cover
   and cook for 4 mins.

2. Meanwhile, cut four rectangles of greaseproof paper, each
   large enough to wrap one piece of fish generously. Brush each
   sheet with a little oil.

3. Put a fish portion in the centre of each sheet of paper and top
   with the vegetables. Sprinkle over any liquid from the
   vegetables.

4. Blend the herbs into the butter and top each pile of vegetables
   with the seasoned butter.

5. Fold the paper over the fish and tuck the short ends
   underneath to form neat parcels. Arrange in a shallow dish.

6. Cook for about 6 mins or until the fish is just cooked. Allow
   to stand for 2-3 mins. Serve the fish in the paper so each
   person can enjoy the delicious aroma as the individual parcels
   are opened.

FISH WITH SUMMER DRESSING
Serves 4
Cooking: 8 mins on HIGH *(100%)*   *Not suitable for freezing*

**4 fillets of white fish, such as cod or haddock, each
  weighing about 175g (6 oz)**
10ml (2 tsp) lemon juice or white wine vinegar
150g (5 oz) Greek yoghurt
2.5ml (½ tsp) concentrated mint sauce
**10cm (4 in) piece of cucumber, skinned, seeds removed
  and diced**
50g (2 oz) seedless green grapes, halved
salt and pepper
thin cucumber slices to garnish

1. Arrange the fish fillets in a shallow dish and sprinkle with the
   lemon juice or vinegar. Cover and cook for 5 mins.

2. Mix together the yoghurt, mint sauce and cucumber. Reserve
   some grapes for garnish, then stir the remainder into the
   yoghurt mixture. Season lightly with salt and pepper. Spread
   evenly over the fish.

3. Cook for a further 3 mins or until the fish is just cooked.
   Allow to stand for 2-3 mins. Serve, garnished with cucumber
   slices and the reserved grapes.

SALMON WITH CREAMY CHIVE SAUCE

Cooking: 10 mins on HIGH (100%)   *Serves 2*
Not suitable for freezing

2 salmon cutlets or fillets
150ml (¼ pt) vegetable stock
100ml (4 fl oz) dry white vermouth
15ml (1 tbsp) lemon juice
30ml (2 tbsp) chopped chives
75ml (5 tbsp) double cream
salt and pepper

1. Put the salmon in a shallow dish and add the stock and vermouth. Cover and cook for 4 mins or until the fish is just cooked.

2. Lift the salmon on to a serving plate and keep warm.

3. Cook the remaining liquid, uncovered, for 5 mins or until reduced by half. Stir in the lemon juice, chives and cream. Season to taste with salt and pepper, then cook for 30 secs. Serve the sauce with the salmon.

PRAWNS A LA PROVENÇALE

Serves 4

Cooking: 15 mins on HIGH (100%)   *Not suitable for freezing*

10ml (2 tsp) olive oil
1 medium onion, finely chopped
1 garlic clove, crushed
1 green pepper, seeds removed and finely chopped
1 celery stick, finely sliced
30ml (2 tbsp) cornflour
400g can chopped tomatoes
2.5ml (½ tsp) sugar
2.5ml (½ tsp) dried mixed herbs
salt and freshly ground black pepper
350g (12 oz) cooked shelled prawns, thawed if frozen
cooked rice or pasta to serve

1. Put the oil, onion, garlic, pepper and celery in a bowl, cover and cook for 5 mins, stirring once or twice.

2. Stir in the cornflour, then add the tomatoes, sugar, herbs and seasonings. Cover and cook for 8 mins, stirring once or twice.

3. Add the prawns, stir, then cook for 2 mins. Allow to stand for 2-3 mins before serving with rice or pasta.

MARINATED PRAWN KEBABS   *Serves 4*
Cooking: 4 mins on HIGH (100%) plus marinating
Not suitable for freezing

16 large raw prawns, heads removed
45ml (3 tbsp) clear honey
15ml (1 tbsp) lemon juice or white wine vinegar
30ml (2 tbsp) light soy sauce
30ml (2 tbsp) tomato ketchup
green salad and lemon wedges to serve

1. Thread the prawns onto four bamboo skewers, leaving a small gap between each prawn. Lay them in a shallow dish.

2. Mix together the remaining ingredients and pour over the prawns, coating them well. Cover and marinate for about 2 hours, turning the skewers occasionally.

3. Lift the skewers out of the marinade and arrange them on a plate − either around the edge, or like spokes of a wheel.

4. Cook, uncovered, for 3-4 mins, rearranging them half way through, or until the prawns are cooked (they will turn pink).

5. Serve with green salad and lemon wedges.

FISH AND BUTTER BEAN CASSEROLE   *Serves 4*
Cooking: 16 mins on HIGH (100%)   *Not suitable for freezing*

25g (1 oz) butter
1 bunch spring onions, chopped
30ml (2 tbsp) flour
150ml (¼ pt) vegetable or fish stock
300ml (½ pt) milk
60ml (4 tbsp) dry white wine
30ml (2 tbsp) chopped fresh parsley
450g (1 lb) white fish, such as cod, haddock, whiting or
  plaice, skinned and boned
450g (1 lb) smoked fish, such as haddock or cod, skinned
  and boned
415g can butter beans, drained
salt and pepper

1. Put the butter and onions in a large casserole dish, cover and
   cook for 2 mins.

2. Stir in the flour then gradually stir in the stock and milk.
   Cook for 5 mins, stirring frequently, until boiling.

3. Add the wine and parsley. Cut the fish into chunks and add
   to the casserole. Stir in the butter beans and season to taste.

4. Cover and cook for 10 mins, stirring gently once or twice,
   until the fish is cooked. Serve immediately.

LEMON SOLE WITH SMOKED SALMON – see page 46.

HADDOCK AND CORN CHOWDER – see page 40.

TUNA AND TOMATO PASTA – see page 44.

9

SAUCES

Sauces are quick and easy to make in the microwave because they can be cooked in a serving jug or bowl. Even small quantities cook well without sticking or burning, as they often do in a saucepan on the hob. Most sauces reheat well in the microwave too.

Tips for cooking sauces
* Use a jug or bowl which is large enough to allow the sauce to boil up.
* Don't bother to cover the container — you need to stir the sauce often and a cover can be a nuisance.
* Most sauces can be cooked on HIGH (100%), but those containing eggs are best cooked on MEDIUM (50%) or MEDIUM-LOW (30%) to prevent them curdling.
* Stir sauces frequently during cooking to prevent lumps forming.
* To develop the flavour of a cooked sauce (such as tomato sauce), or to thicken or reduce it further, continue cooking, uncovered, on MEDIUM (50%) or MEDIUM-LOW (30%) until the desired flavour and consistency are achieved.
* Reheat sauces on HIGH (100%), stirring occasionally.
* *Frozen sauces* can be reheated straight from the freezer. Put the frozen block in a bowl and cook on HIGH (100%) breaking up the sauce as it thaws. Once it has thawed, stir or whisk the sauce occasionally during reheating.

WHITE SAUCE
Cooking: 7 mins on HIGH (100%)

Serves 4-6
Will freeze

Serve with vegetables, fish or ham.

40g (1½ oz) butter
40g (1½ oz) flour
600ml (1 pt) milk
salt and pepper

1. Put the butter in a bowl or jug. Cook for 1 min until melted.

2. Stir in the flour, then gradually blend in the milk. Season to taste.

3. Cook, uncovered, for 5-6 mins, whisking frequently.

CHEESE SAUCE
Follow the method for WHITE SAUCE and add 75-100g (3-4 oz) grated cheese to the cooked sauce. Stir until melted.

MUSHROOM SAUCE
Follow the method for WHITE SAUCE. At stage 1, add 100g (4 oz) finely sliced or chopped mushrooms to the butter, cover and cook for 2 mins.

MUSTARD SAUCE
Follow the method for WHITE SAUCE. Add 30ml (2 tbsp) ready-made mustard to the cooked sauce.

ONION SAUCE
Follow the method for WHITE SAUCE. At stage 1, add a finely chopped onion to the butter, cover and cook for 3 mins.

PARSLEY SAUCE
Follow the method for WHITE SAUCE and add 30-45ml (2-3 tbsp) chopped parsley to the cooked sauce.

PRAWN SAUCE
Follow the method for WHITE SAUCE. Add 100g (4 oz) small peeled prawns and 15ml (1 tbsp) lemon juice to the cooked sauce. Cook for 1 min.

BREAD SAUCE   *Serves 4-6*
Cooking: 5 mins on HIGH *(100%),*
            10 mins on MEDIUM-LOW *(30%) and*
            5 mins on MEDIUM *(50%)*
Will freeze

Serve with turkey or chicken.

1 small onion, finely sliced
1 bay leaf
6 black peppercorns
2 cloves
pinch of ground nutmeg
300ml (½ pt) milk
50g (2 oz) fresh white breadcrumbs
salt and pepper
25g (1 oz) butter

1. Put the onion, bay leaf, peppercorns, cloves, nutmeg and milk into a large bowl or jug. Cook, uncovered, on HIGH (100%) for 3-5 mins or until just boiling.

2. Cover and continue cooking on MEDIUM-LOW (30%) for 10 mins.

3. Strain and return the milk to the bowl or jug. Stir in the breadcrumbs, season to taste and add butter.

4. Cover and cook on MEDIUM (50%) for 5 mins, stirring occasionally.

CREAMY CURRY SAUCE
Serves 4-6
Cooking: 7 mins on HIGH *(100%) and 10 mins on* MEDIUM *(50%)*
Will freeze

Serve with hard-boiled eggs, vegetables, fish, meat or poultry.

15ml (1 tbsp) oil
1 large onion, finely chopped
1 garlic clove, crushed
1 large eating apple, peeled, cored and chopped
15ml (1 tbsp) flour
300ml (½ pt) vegetable or chicken stock
30ml (2 tbsp) curry paste
15ml (1 tbsp) tomato purée
50g (2 oz) creamed coconut, chopped
15ml (1 tbsp) lemon juice
salt and pepper
150ml (¼ pt) single cream

1. Put the oil, onion and garlic into a bowl or jug, cover and cook for 3 mins.

2. Add the apple and then stir in the flour. Blend in the stock, curry paste, tomato purée and coconut.

3. Cook for 3 mins or until the sauce boils, then cook on MEDIUM (50%) for 10 mins, stirring occasionally.

4. Stir in the lemon juice and season with salt and pepper. Add the cream and cook for 1 min.

BOLOGNESE SAUCE

Serves 4

Cooking: 30 mins on HIGH (100%) *Will freeze*

Serve with pasta or as filling for jacket potatoes (page 107).

15ml (1 tbsp) oil
1 large onion, finely chopped
1 garlic clove, crushed
100g (4 oz) lean streaky bacon, finely chopped
2 medium carrots, finely chopped
450g (1 lb) lean minced beef
150ml (¼ pt) beef stock
30ml (2 tbsp) tomato purée
2.5ml (½ tsp) dried mixed herbs
2.5ml (½ tsp) dried oregano
salt and pepper

1. Put the oil, onion, garlic, bacon and carrots in a large bowl. Cover and cook for 5 mins, stirring once.

2. Break up the minced beef and add to the bowl. Cover and cook for 5 mins, stirring once.

3. Add the remaining ingredients and stir well. Cover and cook for 15-20 mins, stirring occasionally.

BARBECUE SAUCE
Cooking: 15 mins on HIGH *(100%)*

Serves 4-6
Will freeze

Serve with burgers, steaks, poultry or vegetables.

15ml (1 tbsp) oil
1 large onion, finely chopped
300ml (½ pt) vegetable stock
45ml (3 tbsp) red wine vinegar
45ml (3 tbsp) brown sugar
45ml (3 tbsp) tomato purée
45ml (3 tbsp) Worcestershire sauce
15ml (1 tbsp) ready-made mustard
5ml (1 tsp) dried mixed herbs
salt and pepper

1. Put the oil and onion in a bowl, cover and cook for 5 mins, stirring once.

2. Stir in the remaining ingredients, cover and cook for 8 mins, stirring once or twice. For a thicker sauce, uncover and continue cooking, stirring occasionally, until the required consistency is achieved.

APPLE SAUCE
Cooking: 5 mins on HIGH *(100%)*

Serves 4
Will freeze

Serve with roast pork, duck or goose.

225g (8 oz) cooking apples, peeled, cored and sliced
10ml (2 tsp) caster sugar (optional)
small knob of butter

1. Put the apples in a bowl with 15ml (1 tbsp) water and the sugar (optional).

2. Cover and cook for 5 mins, stirring occasionally, or until the apples are soft and partially puréed.

3. Stir in the butter and serve hot or cold.

TOMATO SAUCE

Cooking: 13 mins on HIGH (100%)   *Serves 4-6*
                                                     Will freeze

Serve with pasta, vegetables, fish, meat or poultry.

10ml (2 tsp) oil
1 small onion, finely chopped
1 small carrot, finely chopped
1 garlic clove, crushed
15ml (1 tbsp) cornflour
400g can chopped tomatoes or 450g (1 lb) fresh ripe
  tomatoes, skinned and chopped
300ml (½ pt) chicken or vegetable stock
15ml (1 tbsp) sugar
15ml (1 tbsp) tomato purée
salt and freshly ground black pepper

1. Put the oil, onion, carrot and garlic in a bowl or jug, cover and cook for 3 mins.

2. Stir in the cornflour, then add the remaining ingredients.

3. Cover and cook for 10 mins, stirring occasionally.

JAM SAUCE

Cooking: 4 mins on HIGH (100%)   *Serves 4*
                                                     Will freeze

Serve hot with sponge puddings; hot or cold with ice cream.

60ml (4 tbsp) jam
10ml (2 tsp) cornflour

1. Put the jam in a bowl or jug and add 150ml (¼ pt) water. Cook for 2 mins and stir well until the jam melts.

2. Mix the cornflour to a smooth paste with a little water. Stir into the jam mixture.

3. Cook for 2 mins, stirring frequently, until the sauce thickens and boils.

HOLLANDAISE SAUCE
Cooking: 2 mins on HIGH *(100%)*   *Serves 4*
    Not suitable for freezing

Serve with fish (salmon is a favourite) or vegetables (asparagus is traditional).

100g (4 oz) butter
30ml (2 tbsp) white wine vinegar
2 egg yolks
salt and pepper

1. Cut the butter into small pieces and put into a bowl. Cook for ½-1 min until just melted (stir to help it melt if necessary — the butter must not get too hot).

2. Add the vinegar, egg yolks and a little seasoning. Whisk well.

3. Cook, whisking after every 15 secs, until the sauce thickens. Take care not to over-cook or the sauce will curdle.

CHOCOLATE SAUCE
Cooking: 3 mins on MEDIUM *(50%)*   *Serves 4-6*
    Will freeze

Serve with ice cream, chocolate sponge pudding, bananas or poached pears.

175g (6 oz) plain chocolate
45ml (3 tbsp) golden syrup
25g (1 oz) butter
15ml (1 tbsp) lemon juice

1. Break the chocolate into a bowl. Add the remaining ingredients plus 30ml (2 tbsp) water.

2. Cook, uncovered, on MEDIUM (50%) for 3 mins, stirring occasionally, until melted, smooth and glossy.

SWEET WHITE SAUCE
Cooking: 4 mins on HIGH (100%)

Serves 4
Will freeze

Serve with sponge and fruit puddings.

15g (½ oz) cornflour
300ml (½ pt) milk
knob of butter
15ml (1 tbsp) caster sugar
few drops of vanilla essence

1. In a bowl or jug, mix the cornflour to a smooth paste with a little of the milk.

2. Heat the remaining milk for 2 mins. Pour on to the cornflour mixture and whisk well.

3. Cook for 2 mins, whisking frequently, until the sauce thickens and boils.

4. Stir in butter, sugar and vanilla essence.

BRANDY SAUCE
Follow method for SWEET WHITE SAUCE. At stage 4, add 30ml (2 tbsp) brandy.

SUMMER FRUIT SAUCE
Cooking: 8 mins on HIGH (100%)

Serves 6
Will freeze

Serve with ice cream, poached fruit or sponge puddings.

225g (8 oz) frozen summer fruit
175g (6 oz) redcurrant jelly
50ml (2 fl oz) port
10ml (2 tsp) cornflour

1. Put the fruit in a bowl and cook for 3 mins, stirring once, until thawed.

2. Add the jelly and port. Cook for 4 mins, stirring frequently, or until the jelly has melted.

3. Mix the cornflour to a smooth paste with a little water. Add a little of the warm fruit then stir the mixture into the bowl.

4. Cook for 1 min or until the sauce thickens and boils.

BUTTERSCOTCH SAUCE
Cooking: 3½ mins on HIGH (100%)

Serves 4
Will freeze

Serve with ice cream or sponge puddings.

50g (2 oz) butter
50g (2 oz) brown sugar
175g (6 oz) golden syrup
10ml (2 tsp) lemon juice
150ml (¼ pt) double cream

1. Put the butter, sugar and syrup into a bowl or jug and cook for 2-3 mins until melted.

2. Stir until well blended.

3. Stir in the lemon juice and cream. Heat for 30 secs before serving.

10

MEAT AND POULTRY

Meat and poultry can be thawed and cooked in the microwave oven. It is particularly suitable for bacon rashers and joints; whole poultry and poultry pieces; minced meat; and cubes of beef, pork, lamb, bacon and poultry for cooking in a sauce.

The results with joints of meat, chops and steaks depend on personal taste, unless you have a combination oven (which browns and crisps as well as cooking quickly with microwaves). Here, you will find plenty of tips on how to get the best results.

Tips for thawing meat and poultry

* Remove any metal tags from the wrappings.

* Stand the meat or poultry on a microwave or roasting rack — to lift it above the liquid which collects beneath.

* Thaw on DEFROST or MEDIUM-LOW (30%).

* Separate items like bacon rashers, chops and steaks as they begin to thaw. Reposition them occasionally too.

* Turn large pieces, joints and whole birds over at least once during thawing.

* Pour away any moisture as it collects around the meat or poultry during thawing. If you don't, the liquid will heat up while the rest remains frozen.

* If any areas begin to warm up, stop thawing and allow a standing period of about 20 mins before continuing.

* When thawing is completed, allow small pieces to stand for at least 10 mins before cooking. Large pieces, whole poultry and joints need at least 30 mins.

Guide to thawing times	
Per 450g (1 lb) on DEFROST or MEDIUM-LOW (30%)	
Beef joints, on bone boneless Beef, steak	10-12 mins 8-10 mins 8-10 mins
Lamb joints	5-6 mins
Pork/bacon joints	7-8 mins
Chops	8-10 mins
Cubed & minced meat	7-10 mins
Liver & kidney	7-9 mins
Chicken, whole	6-8 mins
Turkey, whole	10-12 mins
Chicken & turkey portions	5-7 mins

Tips for cooking meat and poultry

* Thaw meat and poultry completely before cooking.

* Regular shapes, such as boned and rolled joints, cook more evenly than irregular shapes, such as a leg joint.

* Meat on the bone cooks more quickly than off the bone.

* Secure large items with string or with wooden (not metal) skewers.

* Season with salt after cooking, to prevent the surface from drying and shrinking. If the meat or poultry is immersed in liquid, a little salt can be added prior to cooking.

* Put large pieces and joints on a microwave or roasting rack, so they do not sit in their juices during cooking.

* A browning dish is useful for cooking chops and sausages (follow the dish manufacturer's instructions).

* Arrange small pieces, like chops or chicken drumsticks, with their thinner ends towards the centre of the dish.

* Arrange small even-shaped pieces, such as meatballs, around the edge of the dish.

* Meat loaves cook best in a ring-shaped mould.

* Cover during cooking to keep moisture in, to help the meat or poultry to cook evenly, and to keep the oven walls free from splashes.

* Cover joints or whole poultry with a split roasting bag, to encourage a little browning of the surface.

* Joints and whole poultry are usually cooked on HIGH (100%) (see ** in cooking guide on page 74). Meat and poultry which is immersed in liquid can be brought to the

boil on HIGH (100%), then cooked on MEDIUM (50%) or MEDIUM-LOW (30%) until the meat or poultry is tender — just like boiling and simmering on the hob.

* Turn large pieces, whole poultry and joints at least once during cooking.

* Stir casserole-style dishes occasionally during cooking.

* Check that meat and poultry is cooked by inserting a skewer into the thickest part. The juices should always run clear from pork and poultry, though you may prefer them pink in beef and lamb. If you use a meat thermometer, insert it into the thickest part of the meat and make sure it does not touch any bone.

* Allow joints and whole poultry to stand for 15-20 mins after cooking — to allow the temperature to even out and to make carving easier.

Guide to cooking times

	Per 450g (1 lb) on HIGH (100%)
Beef, rare	5-6 mins
medium	6-7 mins
well done	8-9 mins
Lamb, medium	7-8 mins
well done	8-10 mins
Pork	8-10 mins
Bacon	9-12 mins
Liver and kidney	6-8 mins
Chicken, whole	8-10 mins
Turkey, whole	9-11 mins
Chicken and turkey portions	6-8 mins

** If you find that meat and poultry cooked on HIGH (100%) overcooks, try cooking on HIGH (100%) for the first few minutes, then reducing the power to MEDIUM-HIGH (75%) or MEDIUM (50%) until cooked through.

	on HIGH (100%)
Chops, 1	2-4 mins
2	3-5 mins
3	4-6 mins
4	5-7 mins
Bacon rashers, 2	2-3 mins
4	4-5 mins
6	5-6 mins
Chicken breast, boneless	2-3 mins

BEEF IN STOUT
Serves 4

Cooking: 15 mins on HIGH *(100%) and*
1¼-1½ hrs on MEDIUM-LOW *(30%)*   *Will freeze*

2 rashers lean streaky bacon
225g (8 oz) leeks, thinly sliced
2 celery sticks, thinly sliced
25g (1 oz) flour
salt and pepper
700g (1½ lb) lean braising beef, cubed
2 beef stock cubes
300ml (½ pt) stout
175g (6 oz) no-soak ready-to-eat prunes, stoned
30ml (2 tbsp) tomato purée
5ml (1 tsp) dried mixed herbs

1. Put the bacon, leeks and celery in a large casserole, cover and cook for 5 mins, stirring once.

2. Meanwhile, season the flour with salt and pepper and toss the beef in it until well coated. Stir the beef and any excess flour into the vegetables.

3. Dissolve the stock cubes in 60ml (4 tbsp) boiling water and add to the casserole with the remaining ingredients. Stir well.

4. Cover and cook for 10 mins or until boiling. Continue cooking on MEDIUM-LOW (30%) for 1¼-1½ hrs, stirring occasionally, until the beef is tender.

BEEF AND VEGETABLE CASSEROLE   *Serves 4*

Cooking: 15 mins on HIGH *(100%) and*
         1-1½ hrs on MEDIUM-LOW *(30%)*   *Will freeze*

10ml (2 tsp) oil
1 medium onion, sliced
2 celery sticks, sliced
225g (8 oz) carrots, sliced
225g (8 oz) parsnip, swede or turnip, chopped
450g (1 lb) lean braising beef, cubed
30ml (2 tbsp) flour
300ml (½ pt) beef stock
15ml (1 tbsp) mixed dried herbs
10ml (2 tsp) mustard powder
30ml (2 tbsp) tomato purée
salt and pepper

1. Put the oil and vegetables into a large casserole dish, cover and cook for 5 mins, stirring once.

2. Add the beef, cover and cook for 5 mins, stirring once.

3. Stir in the flour, then add the remaining ingredients.

4. Cover and cook for 5 mins, then continue cooking, covered, on MEDIUM-LOW (30%) for 1-1½ hrs, stirring occasionally, until the beef is tender.

BEEF WITH GINGER AND SPRING ONIONS
Serves 2

Cooking: 6 mins on HIGH (100%) plus marinating
Not suitable for freezing

350g (12 oz) fillet steak
15ml (1 tbsp) finely grated fresh root ginger
1 garlic clove, crushed
60ml (4 tbsp) dry sherry
60ml (4 tbsp) light soy sauce
5ml (1 tsp) clear honey
10ml (2 tsp) oil
20ml (4 tsp) cornflour
1 bunch spring onions, thickly sliced
cooked rice to serve

1. Cut the steak into thin strips across the grain and put into a bowl. Mix together the ginger, garlic, sherry, soy sauce and honey. Pour the mixture over the steak, stirring to coat it well. Cover and marinate in a cool place for 1 hour or more.

2. Put the oil into a large bowl. Use a slotted spoon to lift the steak out of its marinade and stir the steak into the oil. Cook, uncovered for 2 mins, or until the steak is just cooked, stirring once.

3. Whisk the cornflour into the marinade and pour over the steak.

4. Add the onions and cook, uncovered, for 3-4 mins, stirring frequently, until the sauce thickens and boils. Serve with rice.

ALL SEASONS BEEF PIE

Serves 4

Cooking: 15 mins on HIGH (100%) and
20-30 mins on MEDIUM (50%)   *Will freeze*
plus grilling

10ml (2 tsp) oil
2 medium onions, finely chopped
450g (1 lb) lean minced beef
1 beef stock cube
198g can sweetcorn with peppers
15ml (1 tbsp) dried mixed herbs
30ml (2 tbsp) tomato purée
10ml (2 tsp) flour
salt and pepper
450g (1 lb) potatoes, thinly sliced
25g (1 oz) butter

1. Put the oil and onions in a large bowl, cover and cook for 5 mins, stirring once.

2. Break up the beef and stir into the onions. Add the crumbled stock cube, sweetcorn with peppers, herbs, tomato purée, flour and seasoning. Stir well.

3. Cover and cook for 10 mins, stirring twice.

4. Empty the beef mixture into a flameproof dish. Arrange the potatoes on top, seasoning the layers lightly with salt and pepper.

5. Put the butter in a small bowl, cook for 30 secs or until melted and brush it over the top of the potatoes. Cover and cook on MEDIUM (50%) for 20-30 mins until the potatoes are cooked through (test with a skewer or knife).

6. Before serving, put under a hot grill to brown and crisp the top.

MEATBALLS IN SPICY SAUCE

Serves 4

Cooking: 6 mins on HIGH (100%) and
10-15 mins on MEDIUM (50%)

Will freeze

450g (1 lb) lean minced beef
1 small onion, finely chopped
15ml (1 tbsp) dried mixed herbs
1 egg, beaten
150ml (¼ pt) beef stock
15ml (1 tbsp) horseradish sauce
15ml (1 tbsp) Worcestershire sauce
15ml (1 tbsp) tomato purée
10ml (2 tsp) cornflour
few drops of hot chilli sauce
salt and pepper

1. Mix together the beef, onion, herbs and egg and shape into
   16 balls. Arrange them in a large shallow dish and cook,
   uncovered for 6 mins, rearranging them half way through
   cooking.

2. Whisk together the remaining ingredients and pour over and
   around the meatballs. Cover and cook on MEDIUM (50%)
   for 10-15 mins, stirring gently occasionally.

LAMB CURRY

Serves 4

Cooking: 10 mins on HIGH (100%) and
          25 mins on MEDIUM (50%)   *Will freeze*

1 medium onion, sliced
2 garlic cloves, crushed
30ml (2 tbsp) curry powder
700g (1½ lb) fillet or leg of lamb, cubed
400g can chopped tomatoes
1 lamb or beef stock cube
salt and pepper
cooked rice, poppadums (see below) and
**   mango chutney, to serve**

1. Put the onion and garlic in a large bowl, cover and cook for 3 mins.

2. Meanwhile, sprinkle the curry powder over the lamb and toss to coat the cubes well.

3. Stir the lamb into the onion. Add the tomatoes and crumble in the stock cube.

4. Cover and cook for 7 mins or until boiling, stirring once or twice. Continue cooking on MEDIUM (50%) for about 25 mins, stirring occasionally, until the lamb is tender. Half way through cooking, season to taste and remove the lid so that the sauce reduces and thickens.

POPPADUMS

With oil:

Brush one poppadum on one side with a little oil and place it on a sheet of paper towel. Cook for 1 min until crisp and puffed up.

Without oil:

Put two poppadums on a sheet of paper towel and cook for 1-1½ mins until crisp and puffed up.

LAMB WITH SPICED MINT SAUCE

Serves 4

Cooking: 13 mins on HIGH (100%) and
20 mins on MEDIUM (50%)

Will freeze

1 medium onion, thinly sliced
2.5ml (½ tsp) ground coriander
2.5ml (½ tsp) ground cumin
450g (1 lb) fillet or leg of lamb, thinly sliced
350g (12 oz) button mushrooms
15ml (1 tbsp) flour
150ml (¼ pt) lamb or chicken stock
30ml (2 tbsp) white wine vinegar
45ml (3 tbsp) mint jelly
natural yoghurt, to serve

1. Put the onion in a large bowl, cover and cook for 3 mins.

2. Meanwhile, sprinkle the spices over the lamb and toss to coat the slices well.

3. Add the lamb to the onion and stir in the mushrooms. Cover and cook for 5 mins, stirring once or twice.

4. Stir in the flour, then gradually add the stock. Add the vinegar and the mint jelly.

5. Cook for 5 mins, stirring once or twice, or until boiling. Cover and continue cooking on MEDIUM (50%) for 20 mins, stirring occasionally, until the lamb is tender.

6. Serve, topped with a spoonful or two of yoghurt.

MEDITERRANEAN LAMB

Serves 4

Cooking: 14 mins on HIGH (100%) and
20 mins on MEDIUM (50%)

Will freeze

10ml (2 tsp) olive oil
1 medium onion, thinly sliced
15ml (1 tbsp) sugar
1 large aubergine, cubed
100g (4 oz) button mushrooms, thickly sliced
1 red pepper, seeded and sliced
450g (1 lb) fillet or leg of lamb, thinly sliced
150ml (¼ pt) lamb stock
150ml (¼ pt) red wine
30ml (2 tbsp) tomato purée
5ml (1 tsp) dried oregano
salt and pepper
cooked rice or pasta, to serve

1. Put the oil, onion and sugar in a large bowl, cover and cook
   for 3 mins.

2. Add the aubergine, mushrooms and pepper. Cover and cook
   for 3 mins.

3. Stir in the lamb, then add the stock, wine, tomato purée,
   oregano and seasoning.

4. Cover and cook for 8 mins, stirring once or twice, or until
   boiling. Continue cooking, covered, on MEDIUM (50%) for
   20 mins, stirring occasionally, until the lamb is tender.

5. Serve with rice or pasta.

LAMB KORMA

Serves 4

*Cooking: 8 mins on HIGH (100%) and
20 mins on MEDIUM (50%)*

Will freeze

100g (4 oz) ground almonds
30ml (2 tbsp) mild curry paste
10ml (2 tsp) oil
1 medium onion, finely chopped
700g (1½ lb) fillet or leg of lamb, cubed
75ml (3 fl oz) thick natural yoghurt
salt and pepper
75ml (3 fl oz) double cream
lemon wedges, to serve

1. Mix the almonds and curry paste with 150ml (¼ pt) water to make a smooth paste.

2. Put the oil and onion in a large bowl, cover and cook for 3 mins.

3. Add the lamb and stir in the nut paste and yoghurt. Season with salt and pepper.

4. Cover and cook for 5 mins, stirring once or twice. Continue cooking, covered, on MEDIUM (50%) for 20 mins, stirring occasionally, until the lamb is tender.

5. Stir in the cream and serve with lemon wedges.

KOFTAS IN CURRY SAUCE

Serves 4

Cooking: 13 mins on HIGH (100%) and
*   15 mins on MEDIUM (50%)*
Will freeze without the yoghurt

450g (1 lb) lean minced lamb
1 medium onion, finely chopped
2 garlic cloves, crushed
2cm (¾ inch) fresh root ginger, peeled and grated
1 fresh green chilli, seeded and finely chopped
30ml (2 tbsp) chopped fresh coriander or parsley
1 egg, beaten
5ml (1 tsp) oil
10ml (2 tsp) ground coriander
5ml (1 tsp) ground cumin
2.5ml (½ tsp) ground turmeric
2.5ml (½ tsp) ground cinnamon
300ml (½ pt) lamb or beef stock
30ml (2 tbsp) tomato purée
150ml (¼ pt) natural yoghurt

1. Mix together the lamb, half the onion, garlic, ginger, chilli, herbs and egg. Shape the mixture into 16 small balls (koftas).

2. Arrange the meatballs in a large shallow dish. Cook, uncovered, for 5 mins, rearranging them once during cooking. Lift them out of the dish and set aside.

3. Put the remaining onion in the dish with the oil. Cover and cook for 3 mins.

4. Stir in the spices, stock and tomato purée. Cover and cook for 5 mins or until boiling.

5. Add the meatballs (plus their juices) to the dish and coat them with the sauce. Cook, uncovered, on MEDIUM (50%) for 15 mins, rearranging the meatballs once during cooking.

6. Stir in the yoghurt before serving.

PORK IN SWEET AND SOUR SAUCE

Serves 4
Cooking: 17 mins on HIGH (100%)   *Will freeze*

227g can pineapple cubes in fruit juice
chicken or vegetable stock
5ml (1 tsp) oil
1 medium onion, finely sliced
1 garlic clove, crushed
2 celery sticks, finely sliced
450g (1 lb) lean pork, finely sliced
30ml (2 tbsp) tomato purée
45ml (3 tbsp) red wine vinegar
45ml (3 tbsp) soy sauce
45ml (3 tbsp) brown sugar
30ml (2 tbsp) cornflour
salt and pepper
1 green pepper, seeded and finely sliced

1. Drain the pineapple and make up the juice to 300ml (½ pt) with chicken or vegetable stock.

2. Put the oil, onion, garlic and celery in a large bowl. Cover and cook for 5 mins, stirring once.

3. Stir in the pork and the pineapple-juice mixture.

4. Whisk together the tomato purée, vinegar, soy sauce, sugar and cornflour, then stir into the pork mixture. Season with salt and pepper.

5. Cover and cook for 5 mins, stirring once, or until boiling. Continue cooking, covered, for 5 mins, stirring twice, or until the pork is tender.

6. Stir in the pepper and pineapple, cover and cook for 2 mins until hot.

PORK AND BEAN CASSEROLE

Serves 4-6

Cooking: 13 mins on HIGH *(100%) and*
20-30 mins on MEDIUM *(50%)*

Will freeze

15g (½ oz) butter
5ml (1 tsp) oil
1 large onion, finely sliced
700g (1½ lb) lean pork, cubed
400g can chopped tomatoes
1 chicken stock cube
15ml (1 tbsp) tomato purée
5ml (1 tsp) dried mixed herbs
salt and pepper
415g can red kidney beans, drained

1. Put the butter, oil and onion in a large bowl, cover and cook for 5 mins, stirring once.

2. Stir in the pork. Add the remaining ingredients and stir well.

3. Cover and cook for 8 mins, stirring once or twice, or until boiling. Continue cooking, covered, on MEDIUM (50%) for 20-30 mins, stirring occasionally, until the pork is tender.

CHILLI PORK AND BEANS

Serves 4

Cooking: 14 mins on HIGH *(100%) and*
20 mins on MEDIUM *(50%)*

Will freeze

1 medium onion, finely chopped
1 garlic clove, crushed
450g (1 lb) pork fillet or tenderloin, thinly sliced
30ml (2 tbsp) flour
5ml (1 tsp) chilli powder
2.5ml (½ tsp) ground cumin
150ml (¼ pt) chicken, beef or vegetable stock
400g can chopped tomatoes
415g can red kidney beans, drained
salt and pepper

1. Put the onion and garlic in a large bowl, cover and cook for 3 mins.

2. Stir in the pork, cover and cook for 3 mins.

3. Stir in the flour, then add the remaining ingredients.

4. Cover and cook for 8 mins, stirring once or twice, or until boiling. Continue cooking on MEDIUM (50%) for 20 mins, stirring occasionally, or until the pork is tender. Remove the lid half way through cooking to reduce and thicken the sauce.

PORK ORIENTAL   *Serves 4*
Cooking: 20 mins on HIGH (100%) plus marinating
Will freeze

30ml (2 tbsp) soy sauce
15ml (1 tbsp) Worcestershire sauce
60ml (4 tbsp) tomato ketchup
15ml (1 tbsp) brown sugar
15ml (1 tbsp) coarse-grain mustard
450g (1 lb) pork fillet or tenderloin, thinly sliced
1 medium onion, thinly sliced
150ml (¼ pt) chicken or vegetable stock
1 red pepper, seeded and sliced
100g (4 oz) mushrooms, thickly sliced

1. Mix together the soy sauce, Worcestershire sauce, ketchup, sugar and mustard. Add the pork and stir to coat it well. Cover and allow to marinate in a cool place for 30 mins-2 hrs.

2. Put the onion in a large bowl, cover and cook for 3 mins.

3. Lift the pork out of its marinade and stir the meat into the onion. Cook, uncovered, for 7 mins, stirring once or twice.

4. Add the marinade and stock. Cook, uncovered, for 5 mins.

5. Stir in the pepper and mushrooms and cook, uncovered for 5 mins.

SPARE RIBS BARBECUE-STYLE

Serves 4

Cooking: 10 mins on HIGH (100%) and
25 mins on MEDIUM (50%) plus marinating

Will freeze

1 small onion, finely chopped
60ml (4 tbsp) tomato ketchup
60ml (4 tbsp) Worcestershire sauce
15ml (1 tbsp) malt vinegar
10ml (2 tsp) brown sugar
5ml (1 tsp) mustard powder
2.5ml (½ tsp) paprika
900g (2 lb) small lean pork spare ribs

1. To make the marinade, mix together the onion, ketchup, Worcestershire sauce, vinegar, sugar, mustard and paprika. Coat the spare ribs with the mixture and arrange them in a large shallow dish, pouring over any extra marinade. Cover and allow to marinate in a cool place for 1-2 hrs.

2. Cover and cook for 10 mins, then cook on MEDIUM (50%) for a further 10 mins.

3. Rearrange the ribs, then cook uncovered on MEDIUM (50%) for a further 15 mins, turning them once or twice, or until they are tender.

BACON HOTPOT
Serves 4

Cooking: 20 mins on HIGH (100%) and
*   20 mins on MEDIUM-LOW (30%) plus grilling*
Not suitable for freezing

25g (1 oz) butter
1 medium onion, thinly sliced
225g (8 oz) carrots, thickly sliced
3 celery sticks, chopped
550g (1¼ lb) lean unsmoked bacon joint, cubed
30ml (2 tbsp) flour
300ml (½ pt) dry cider
15ml (1 tbsp) coarse-grain mustard
salt and pepper
450g (1 lb) potatoes, thinly sliced

1. Put half the butter in a large flameproof casserole dish with the onion, carrots and celery. Cover and cook for 5 mins, stirring once.

2. Add the bacon, sprinkle the flour over and stir well. Add the cider, mustard and seasoning.

3. Cover and cook for 10 mins, stirring once or twice, or until boiling.

4. Arrange the potato slices on top, seasoning each layer lightly with salt and pepper. Cover and cook for 5 mins, then continue cooking on MEDIUM-LOW (30%) for 20 mins or until the bacon and potatoes are tender.

5. Put the remaining butter in a small bowl and cook for 30 secs until melted. Brush the melted butter over the potatoes.

6. Put under a hot grill until crisp and golden brown.

AUTUMN BACON CASSEROLE
Serves 4

Cooking: 15 mins on HIGH *(100%) and*
30 mins on MEDIUM *(50%)*   *Will freeze*

15g (½ oz) butter
12 tiny onions
450g (1 lb) lean bacon joint, cubed
30ml (2 tbsp) flour
300ml (½ pt) bacon, chicken or vegetable stock
2 medium leeks, sliced
1 large carrot, thinly sliced
400g can tomatoes
50g (2 oz) canned or frozen sweetcorn kernels
freshly ground black pepper

1. Put the butter and onions into a large bowl, cover and cook
   for 5 mins, stirring once.

2. Add the bacon and stir in the flour. Gradually stir in the
   stock, then add the remaining ingredients.

3. Cover and cook for 8-10 mins, stirring once or twice, or
   until boiling. Continue cooking, covered, on MEDIUM
   (50%) for 30 mins, stirring occasionally, until the bacon is
   tender.

ORANGE-GLAZED GAMMON

Serves 8

Cooking: 15 mins on HIGH *(100%) and*
45 mins on MEDIUM *(50%) plus grilling*
Will freeze

1.4kg (3 lb) gammon joint
45ml (3 tbsp) fine-cut orange marmalade
45ml (3 tbsp) demerara sugar

1. Put the gammon in a large bowl and pour over sufficient boiling water to cover it. Cover and cook for 5 mins. Allow to stand for 5 mins, then discard the water.

2. Pour over sufficient boiling water to cover the gammon again. Cover and cook for 10 mins. Turn the joint over, cover and continue cooking on MEDIUM (50%) for about 45 mins, turning the gammon once, until cooked through.

3. Allow to stand for 10 mins, then drain off the stock (why not reserve it and make it into a delicious soup?). Cut the skin off the gammon and slash the fat lightly with a sharp knife (a striped or diamond pattern looks good).

4. Mix together the marmalade and sugar and spread the mixture over the fat surface. Cook under a hot grill until golden brown and bubbling hot.

LIVER AND APPLE CASSEROLE

Serves 4

Cooking: 10 mins on HIGH *(100%) and*
5-10 mins on MEDIUM *(50%)*
Not suitable for freezing

15g (½ oz) butter
1 medium onion, thinly sliced
1 medium carrot, thinly sliced
450g (1 lb) lamb's liver, thinly sliced
30ml (2 tbsp) flour
salt and freshly ground black pepper
2.5ml (½ tsp) dried sage or
    5ml (1 tsp) chopped fresh sage
450ml (¾ pt) boiling lamb or beef stock
2 eating apples, cored and sliced

1. Put the butter, onion and carrot in a large bowl. Cover and cook for 5 mins, stirring once.

2. Add the liver. Stir in the flour, seasoning and sage. Gradually stir in the boiling stock. Cover and cook for 5 mins or until boiling.

3. Add the apples, cover and cook on MEDIUM (50%) for 5-10 mins, stirring once, until the liver is just tender.

CHICKEN IN MUSTARD SAUCE   *Serves 4*
Cooking: 10 mins on HIGH *(100%) and*
*   15 mins on* MEDIUM *(50%)*   *Will freeze*

15g (½ oz) butter
1 medium onion, sliced
2 medium leeks, sliced
8 chicken thighs, skinned
150ml (¼ pt) chicken stock
150ml (¼ pt) dry white wine
30ml (2 tbsp) French mustard
salt and pepper
100g (4 oz) button mushrooms, sliced

1. Put the butter, onion and leeks in a large bowl. Cover and cook for 5 mins. Stir well.

2. Arrange the chicken in a circle on top of the vegetables.

3. Mix together the stock, wine, mustard and seasoning. Stir in the mushrooms and pour over the chicken.

4. Cover and cook for 5 mins, then continue cooking on MEDIUM (50%) for 15 mins, spooning the sauce over the chicken occasionally during cooking.

CHICKEN IN ORANGE

Cooking: 10-15 mins on HIGH (100%)

Serves 4
Will freeze

10ml (2 tsp) oil
550g (1¼ lb) boneless chicken breasts,
  skinned and sliced
10ml (2 tsp) cornflour
grated rind and juice of 1 large orange
1 chicken or vegetable stock cube
15ml (1 tbsp) dark soy sauce
15ml (1 tbsp) clear honey
1 bunch spring onions, sliced
salt and pepper
orange slices, to garnish

1. Put the oil and chicken into a medium bowl. Cover and cook for 5 mins, stirring once.

2. Blend the cornflour with the orange juice and the crumbled stock cube. Stir in the orange rind, soy sauce, honey and spring onions. Pour the sauce over the chicken.

3. Cover and cook for 5-10 mins, stirring occasionally, until the sauce thickens and boils and the chicken is tender.

4. Season to taste and serve, garnished with orange slices.

CHICKEN CHASSEUR

Serves 4

*Cooking: 11 mins on HIGH (100%) and
20 mins on MEDIUM (50%)*

Will freeze

25g (1 oz) butter
1 medium onion, finely chopped
30ml (2 tbsp) flour
150ml (¼ pt) dry white wine
300ml (½ pt) boiling chicken stock
salt and freshly ground black pepper
4 chicken breasts, skinned
100g (4 oz) button mushrooms
15ml (1 tbsp) chopped fresh parsley

1. Put the butter and onion in a large bowl, cover and cook for
   3 mins. Stir in the flour, then gradually stir in the wine. Add
   the boiling chicken stock, salt and pepper. Cook for 5 mins,
   stirring occasionally, or until the sauce thickens and boils.

2. Add the chicken to the sauce, coating it well. Cover and
   cook on MEDIUM (50%) for 20 mins, stirring occasionally,
   until the chicken is tender.

3. Stir in the mushrooms and parsley, cover and cook for
   3 mins. Allow to stand for 5 mins before serving.

CURRIED CHICKEN

Serves 4

Cooking: 5 mins on HIGH *(100%) and
15 mins on* MEDIUM *(50%)*

Will freeze

10ml (2 tsp) oil
1 large onion, finely chopped
2 garlic cloves, crushed
4 boneless chicken breasts, skinned and thickly sliced
30ml (2 tbsp) curry paste
10ml (2 tsp) flour
15ml (1 tbsp) white wine vinegar
juice of 1 lemon
150ml (¼ pt) chicken stock
cooked rice, poppadums (see page 80) and
  mango chutney, to serve

1. Put the oil, onion and garlic into a medium bowl, cover and cook for 3 mins.

2. Stir in the chicken, cover and cook for 2 mins.

3. Blend the curry paste with the flour, vinegar and lemon juice. Stir into the stock and pour over the chicken.

4. Cover and cook on MEDIUM (50%) for about 15 mins, stirring occasionally, or until the chicken is tender. Serve with rice, poppadums and mango chutney.

ORIENTAL CHICKEN   *Serves 4*
Cooking: 9-13 mins on HIGH *(100%) Not suitable for freezing*

10ml (2 tsp) oil
4 boneless chicken breasts, skinned and thinly sliced
15ml (1 tbsp) grated fresh root ginger
30ml (2 tbsp) soy sauce
30ml (2 tbsp) dry sherry
1 bunch spring onions, sliced
2 red or yellow peppers (or one of each), seeded
** and thinly sliced**
225g can water chestnuts, drained and sliced
30ml (2 tbsp) toasted sesame seeds
few drops sesame oil

1. Put the oil and chicken in a large bowl and mix well. Cover and cook for 3 mins, stirring once.

2. Mix together the ginger, soy sauce and sherry and add to the bowl with the onions, peppers and water chestnuts.

3. Cover and cook for 6-10 mins, stirring occasionally, until the chicken is cooked through.

4. Stir in the sesame seeds and sesame oil before serving.

TURKEY IN TOMATO SAUCE WITH
MUSHROOMS
Serves 4
Cooking: 30 mins on HIGH *(100%)*
Will freeze

45ml (3 tbsp) flour
salt and pepper
700g (1½ lb) boneless turkey fillet, cubed
25g (1 oz) butter
1 large onion, finely chopped
1 garlic clove, crushed
150ml (¼ pt) chicken stock
150ml (¼ pt) dry white vermouth
400g can chopped tomatoes
225g (8 oz) button mushrooms
30ml (2 tsp) chopped parsley

1. Season the flour with salt and pepper. Add the turkey and
   toss to coat it well.

2. Put the butter, onion and garlic into a large bowl. Cover and
   cook for 5 mins, stirring once.

3. Add the turkey to the onion mixture and stir in the stock,
   vermouth and tomatoes. Cover and cook for 15 mins,
   stirring once.

4. Stir in the mushrooms and cook, uncovered, for 10 mins or
   until the turkey is tender and the sauce has reduced slightly.
   Add the parsley just before serving.

11

EGGS AND CHEESE

Eggs and cheese are popular choices for a quick snack, breakfast, lunch or supper. Both do well in the microwave, so long as they are cooked gently and carefully.

Tips for cooking eggs
* Do not try to cook an egg in its shell — steam builds up beneath the shell, making it explode, even after the microwaves have been turned off.
* Eggs which are at room temperature give the best results.
* Prick the yolks of eggs which are to be left whole during cooking, to prevent them from bursting open.
* Avoid overcooking eggs — they become tough. Always stop cooking before the egg or eggs are fully cooked — they will finish cooking during a short standing time.
* If eggs cook too quickly on HIGH (100%), better results may be achieved by using MEDIUM (50%) power.

Tips for cooking cheese
* Add cheese to a dish towards the end of cooking when possible, to prevent it overcooking and becoming stringy.
* Cheese melts quickly and evenly if it is grated rather than sliced or diced.
* If cheese cooks too quickly on HIGH (100%), better results may be achieved by using MEDIUM (50%) power.

BAKED EGGS

1. Break the eggs into small cups, dishes or ramekins. Prick the yolks. Arrange the dishes in a circle in the microwave.

2. Cook on MEDIUM (50%) until almost set:
   1 egg − about 1 min
   2 eggs − about 1½ mins
   3 eggs − about 2 mins
   4 eggs − about 2½ mins.

3. Allow to stand for 1-2 mins before serving.

POACHED EGG

1. Pour 150ml (¼ pt) water into a medium bowl or jug. Add a dash of vinegar. Bring to the boil.

2. Break an egg into the boiling water. Prick the yolk.

3. Cook for ½-1 min.

4. Allow to stand for 1-2 mins before lifting out with a slotted spoon and serving.

SCRAMBLED EGGS   *Serves 2*
Cooking: 2-3 mins on HIGH (100%) Not suitable for freezing

4 eggs
60ml (4 tbsp) milk
25g (1 oz) butter
salt and pepper

1. In a medium bowl or jug, beat together the eggs and milk. Add the butter and season to taste.

2. Cook for 2-3 mins, stirring or whisking frequently (each time the egg sets around the edges of the bowl). Stop cooking when the eggs are still slightly undercooked − they will continue cooking as they are being served.

Note: If you find the eggs cook too quickly on HIGH (100%), reduce the power to MEDIUM (50%).

PIPERADE
Serves 2

Cooking: 7-8 mins on HIGH (100%) Not suitable for freezing

25g (1 oz) butter
1 small onion, finely chopped
1 garlic clove, crushed
1 medium green pepper, seeded and thinly sliced
227g can chopped tomatoes, drained
salt and freshly ground black pepper
4 eggs, beaten

1. Put the butter, onion, garlic and pepper in a medium bowl. Cover and cook for 4 mins.

2. Stir in the tomatoes and season to taste with salt and pepper. Cook, uncovered, for 1 min.

3. Stir in the eggs and cook, uncovered for 2-3 mins, stirring frequently, until the eggs are lightly scrambled.

BACON AND MUSHROOM OMELETTE *Serves 2*

Cooking: 7 mins on HIGH (100%)   Not suitable for freezing

15g (½ oz) butter
2 lean bacon rashers, chopped
50g (2 oz) button mushrooms, thinly sliced
2 spring onions, chopped
4 eggs, beaten
salt and pepper

1. Put the butter and bacon in a shallow dish measuring about 20cm (8 in) in diameter. Cook, uncovered, for 2 mins.

2. Stir in the mushrooms and onions and cook, uncovered, for 1 min.

3. Season the eggs with salt and pepper and pour them over the bacon mixture. Cook, uncovered, for 3-4 mins, until just set, lifting the cooked areas from the sides of the dish after each minute to allow the liquid to run to the edges. Cut into wedges to serve.

EGG AND CHEESE ROLL   *Serves 1*
Cooking: 1½-2 mins on HIGH *(100%) Not suitable for freezing*

1 soft bread roll
15g (½ oz) butter
1 egg
25g (1 oz) grated cheese

1. Cut a slice off the top of the bread roll and reserve. Scoop out the crumbs from the centre of the roll.

2. Put the butter in a small bowl and cook for 30 secs until melted. Brush some butter in the cavity of the roll. Brush the remainder over the cut side of the reserved slice.

3. Break the egg into the roll and prick the yolk. Sprinkle with grated cheese and replace the lid.

4. Cook, uncovered, for 1½-2 mins, or until the egg is just set. Serve hot or cold.

CHEDDAR FONDUE   *Serves 4-6*
Cooking: 6-8 mins on HIGH *(100%) Not suitable for freezing*

1 garlic clove, halved
450g (1 lb) mature Cheddar cheese, grated
15ml (1 tbsp) cornflour
300ml (½ pt) white wine
5ml (1 tsp) lemon juice
25g (1 oz) butter
freshly ground pepper
pinch of ground nutmeg
crusty bread cubes, to serve

1. Rub the inside of a large bowl with the cut sides of the garlic.

2. Add the cheese and cornflour to the bowl and mix well. Stir in the wine, lemon juice and butter.

3. Cook, uncovered, for 6-8 mins, stirring frequently, until the cheese melts and the mixture is thick and smooth.

4. Season with pepper and stir in the nutmeg. Serve with bread cubes − spear them on long forks and dip into the fondue.

EGGS FLORENTINE   *Serves 4*
Cooking: 10 mins on HIGH *(100%) and*
*   4 mins on* MEDIUM *(50%) plus grilling*
Not suitable for freezing

700g (1½ lb) fresh spinach, chopped
25g (1 oz) butter
45ml (3 tbsp) flour
300ml (½ pt) milk
75g (3 oz) mature Cheddar cheese, grated
salt and pepper
4 eggs

1. Put the spinach in a large bowl, cover and cook for 5 mins, stirring once, or until just tender. Drain well.

2. Put the butter, flour and milk in a medium bowl or jug and whisk well. Cook for about 5 mins, whisking frequently, until the sauce thickens and boils. Stir in the cheese and season with salt and pepper.

3. Break the eggs into four small dishes or ramekins and prick the yolks. Cook on MEDIUM (50%) for 3-4 mins, until the egg whites are just set.

4. Put the spinach in a shallow flameproof dish. Slide the eggs out of their dishes, on to the spinach. Pour the cheese sauce over and brown under a hot grill.

12

VEGETABLES

Fresh vegetables cooked in the microwave are simply delicious. Because they are cooked quickly and in the minimum amount of liquid, they retain their full flavour and colour, and cook to the stage where they are still slightly crunchy. Small quantities of vegetables are very successful too, cooked in a small dish so there is no saucepan to wash up.

Cooked vegetables also reheat well in the microwave — to look and taste as if they had only just been cooked.

Tips for cooking vegetables
* Use good quality vegetables for best results. Old, tired vegetables will toughen and dry out.

* Choose even-sized vegetables for cooking whole. Otherwise, cut them into even-sized pieces to encourage even cooking.

* Prick the skins of whole vegetables in several places before cooking, to prevent them bursting open.

* Frozen vegetables can be cooked straight from the freezer.

* Arrange whole vegetables in a circle, to encourage them to cook evenly. Avoid putting one in the centre.

* When cooking more than 450g (1 lb) cut vegetables, best results may be obtained if they are cooked in batches.

* Add 45-60ml (3-4 tbsp) water to the vegetables. Root vegetables and old vegetables often need more. Extra water may also be needed if you want to cook vegetables until they are very soft.

* Season vegetables with salt after cooking or they will become dry and tough.

* Cook most vegetables on HIGH (100%). If they tend to overcook or shrivel, it may be preferable to cook on a slightly lower power, such as MEDIUM-HIGH (75%).

* Cover cut vegetables during cooking to keep the moisture in.

* Stir, shake or turn vegetables occasionally to encourage them to cook evenly.

* Cooking times will depend on the type and quantity of vegetables as well as their age. As a guide, 450g (1 lb) cut vegetables take 7-10 mins. Always underestimate the time and test in the usual way − by inserting the tip of a knife.

* Whole vegetables, such as potatoes, need to stand for several minutes before serving, to allow the temperature to even out.

BLANCHING VEGETABLES

1. Put up to 450g (1 lb) prepared vegetables in a bowl with 45-60ml (3-4 tbsp) water.

2. Cover and cook for 3-4 mins, stirring once, until the vegetables are hot.

3. Drain and tip the vegetables into ice-cold water. Drain them again, then put into polythene bags and freeze.

JACKET POTATOES

1. Scrub and dry potatoes weighing about 175g (6 oz) each. Using a fork, prick their skins in several places. Put them in the microwave, in a circle.

2. Cook, uncovered, until tender:
     5-6   mins for 1
     8-10 mins for 2
     9-12 mins for 3
    10-15 mins for 4.
   Turn them over at least once during cooking.

3. Allow the potatoes to stand for 5 mins before serving.

CARROTS IN ORANGE GLAZE   *Serves 4*
Cooking: 10 mins on HIGH *(100%)   Not suitable for freezing*

450g (1 lb) carrots, thinly sliced
25g (1 oz) butter
75ml (5 tbsp) orange juice
5ml (1 tsp) clear honey
salt and freshly ground black pepper
15ml (1 tbsp) chopped fresh parsley

1. Put the carrots in a large bowl and add the butter, orange juice and honey. Cover and cook for about 10 mins, stirring occasionally, until the carrots are tender.

2. Season to taste and stir in the parsley.

LEEKS PARMESAN   *Serves 4*
Cooking: 14 mins on HIGH *(100%)*
Will freeze — best without the breadcrumbs and cheese

50g (2 oz) butter
50g (2 oz) fresh breadcrumbs
25g (1 oz) Parmesan cheese, finely grated
4 medium leeks, thinly sliced
5ml (1 tsp) soft brown sugar
30ml (2 tbsp) double cream
salt and freshly ground black pepper

1. Put 25g (1 oz) butter in a shallow heatproof container and cook for 30 secs or until melted. Stir in the breadcrumbs, coating them well. Cook, uncovered, for about 4 mins, stirring every minute, until golden brown. Add the cheese.

2. Put the remaining butter, leeks and sugar in a bowl. Cover and cook for about 8 mins, stirring occasionally, until the leeks are just tender.

3. Stir in the cream and season to taste. Cook for 1 min.

4. Tip the leeks and their sauce into a flameproof dish and scatter the breadcrumb mixture over the top. If wished, brown under a hot grill for a few minutes before serving.

PARSLEY BAKED ONIONS   *Serves 4*
Cooking: 10-12 mins on HIGH *(100%) Not suitable for freezing*

350g (12 oz) small or pickling onions, peeled
5ml (1 tsp) lemon juice or white wine vinegar
25g (1 oz) butter
45ml (3 tbsp) chopped fresh parsley
salt and freshly ground black pepper

1. Put all the ingredients in a medium bowl, cover and cook for 10-12 mins, stirring occasionally.

2. Allow to stand for 5 mins before serving.

POTATOES DAUPHINOIS   *Serves 4*
Cooking: 5 mins on HIGH *(100%) and*
*   25 mins on* MEDIUM *(50%) plus grilling*
Not suitable for freezing

700g (1½ lb) potatoes, thinly sliced
50g (2 oz) Cheddar or Gruyère cheese, grated
salt and freshly ground black pepper
150ml (¼ pt) double cream
150ml (¼ pt) milk
1 garlic clove crushed
pinch of ground nutmeg
15g (½ oz) butter

1. Butter a flameproof dish. Layer the potatoes with the cheese in the dish, seasoning each layer lightly.

2. Mix the cream with the milk and add the garlic and nutmeg. Pour evenly over the potatoes. Dot with the butter.

3. Cover and cook for 5 mins.

4. Uncover and cook on MEDIUM (50%) for about 25 mins until the potatoes are tender.

5. Brown under a hot grill.

BEETROOT AND APPLE SALAD
Serves 4
Cooking: 15 mins on HIGH *(100%)*   *Will freeze*

225g (8 oz) beetroot, diced
30ml (2 tbsp) red wine vinegar
5ml (1 tsp) sugar
2 celery sticks, thinly sliced
1 large eating apple, cored and diced

1. Put the beetroot, vinegar and sugar in a bowl with 60ml (4 tbsp) water. Cover and cook for about 15 mins, stirring occasionally, or until the beetroot is tender.

2. Stir in the celery and apples. Serve warm or chilled.

GINGERED CABBAGE
Serves 4
Cooking: 10 mins on HIGH *(100%)*   *Not suitable for freezing*

40g (1½ oz) butter
15ml (1 tbsp) grated fresh root ginger
1 small garlic clove, crushed
450g (1 lb) cabbage, shredded
salt and freshly ground black pepper

1. Put the butter in a large bowl and cook for 45 secs or until melted.

2. Stir in the ginger and garlic. Add the cabbage and stir well to coat it with butter.

3. Cover and cook for about 9 mins, stirring occasionally, or until tender.

4. Season to taste before serving.

VEGETABLES IN CREAM SAUCE
Serves 2 as a main meal, 4 as an accompaniment
Cooking: 10 mins on HIGH (100%)   Not suitable for freezing

25g (1 oz) butter
1 large onion, thinly sliced
4 medium carrots, thinly sliced
4 celery sticks, thinly sliced
225g (8 oz) small broccoli florets
100g (4 oz) button mushrooms
150ml (¼ pt) vegetable stock
15ml (1 tbsp) cornflour
150ml (¼ pt) soured cream
salt and freshly ground black pepper
15ml (1 tbsp) chopped fresh chives
50g (2 oz) toasted cashew nuts or pine nuts

1. Put the butter and onion in a large bowl, cover and cook for 3 mins.

2. Stir in the carrots, celery, broccoli, mushrooms and stock. Cover and cook for about 8 mins, stirring occasionally, until the vegetables are just tender.

3. Mix the cornflour with the cream to make a smooth paste, season to taste and add the chives. Stir into the vegetables. Cook, uncovered, for about 2 mins, stirring once, until the sauce thickens and boils.

4. Scatter the nuts over the top and serve immediately.

RATATOUILLE

Serves 4-6

Cooking: 15 mins on HIGH *(100%) and*
15 mins on MEDIUM *(50%)*

Will freeze

1 medium aubergine, sliced
salt
30ml (2 tbsp) olive oil
1 large onion, thinly sliced
1 large garlic clove, crushed
2 large courgettes, sliced
1 red pepper, seeded and sliced
1 yellow pepper, seeded and sliced
400g can chopped tomatoes
30ml (2 tbsp) chopped fresh herbs, such as thyme,
    basil and/or parsley
30ml (2 tbsp) tomato purée
salt and freshly ground black pepper

1. Sprinkle the aubergine slices with salt, if wished, and allow
   to stand for 30 mins. Rinse and dry well.

2. Put the oil, onion and garlic in a large bowl. Cover and cook
   for 5 mins.

3. Stir in the aubergine slices, courgettes and peppers. Cover
   and cook for 5 mins, stirring once.

4. Add the tomatoes, herbs and tomato purée. Season well.
   Cover and cook for 5 mins, then continue cooking on
   MEDIUM (50%) for 15 mins, stirring gently occasionally.

5. Allow to stand for at least 10 mins before serving hot or
   cold.

MIXED BEAN MEDLEY

Serves 4-6

*Cooking: 7 mins on HIGH (100%) and
10 mins on MEDIUM (50%)*

Will freeze

30ml (2 tbsp) olive oil
1 large onion, thinly sliced
2 garlic cloves, crushed
15ml (1 tbsp) tomato purée
45ml (3 tbsp) chopped fresh herbs, such as thyme,
  oregano, and/or fennel
5ml (1 tsp) sugar
226g can chopped tomatoes
grated rind and juice of 1 lemon
430g can haricot beans, drained
439g can red kidney beans, drained
salt and freshly ground black pepper
salad and garlic bread, to serve

1. Put the oil, onion and garlic in a large bowl, cover and cook for 3 mins.

2. Mix together the tomato purée, herbs, sugar, tomatoes, lemon rind and juice. Pour the sauce over the onion, cover and cook for 4 mins, stirring once, or until boiling.

3. Stir in the beans and season to taste. Cover and cook on MEDIUM (50%) for 10 mins.

4. Serve hot or at room temperature with salad and garlic bread.

CURRIED VEGETABLES

Cooking: 19 mins on HIGH (100%)

Serves 4

Will freeze

30ml (2 tbsp) oil
10ml (2 tsp) ground coriander
5ml (1 tsp) ground cumin
2.5ml (½ tsp) turmeric
2.5ml (½ tsp) chilli powder
1 medium onion, finely chopped
2 garlic cloves, crushed
2 medium potatoes, chopped
2 medium carrots, sliced
1 small cauliflower, cut into small florets
227g can tomatoes
150ml (¼ pt) vegetable stock
2 courgettes, thickly sliced
50g (2 oz) creamed coconut, chopped
salt and pepper
150ml (¼ pt) natural yoghurt
cooked rice, to serve

1. Put the oil, spices, onion and garlic in a large bowl, cover and cook for 1-2 mins, stirring once.

2. Add the potatoes, carrots and cauliflower. Stir well to coat them with the spices.

3. Mix the tomatoes with the vegetable stock and add to the bowl.

4. Cover and cook for 12 mins, stirring gently occasionally.

5. Add the courgettes and coconut, cover and cook for 5 mins, stirring once or twice, until the coconut has melted and the vegetables are tender.

6. Season to taste, stir in the yoghurt and serve with rice.

13

RICE, PASTA, PULSES AND CEREALS

The cooking of rice, pasta and pulses is not necessarily quicker in a microwave. However, microwaving is certainly a convenient and clean method.

Instant breakfast cereals and porridge are quick and convenient too, particularly when individual portions are prepared in the microwave.

Tips for cooking rice, pasta and pulses

* Use a large deep bowl, to allow the contents to boil up.

* Adding a little oil to the cooking water helps to prevent it from boiling over.

* Large quantities, over 450g (1 lb), are best cooked conventionally on the hob.

* Always add boiling water to the rice, pasta or pulses. Boil the water in a kettle to save time.

* Salt can be added to the cooking water of pasta. Rice and pulses are best seasoned with salt after cooking, to prevent them from toughening.

* Though covering during cooking keeps moisture in, results are just as good if no cover is used — and there is less chance of the contents boiling over and flooding the floor of the microwave.

* Stir well after adding the boiling water, before cooking.

* Rice need not be stirred again, but pasta and pulses should be stirred occasionally during cooking.

* Allow a standing time of 5 minutes before serving.

RICE – Basic method
1. Put the rice in a large deep bowl. Pour over boiling water:
      300ml (½ pt) for 100g (4 oz) white rice
      450ml (¾ pt) for 100g (4 oz) brown rice
      600ml (1 pt) for 225g (8 oz) white rice
      750ml (1¼ pt) for 225g (8 oz) brown rice.

2. Stir well. Cook for about 10 mins for white rice, or 20-30 mins for brown rice, until the rice is tender and has absorbed all the water.

3. Season to taste, stir, cover and allow the rice to stand for 5 mins before serving.

PASTA – Basic method

1. Put the pasta in a large deep bowl with salt and a little oil, if wished. Pour over sufficient boiling water to cover the pasta by at least 2.5cm (1 in). Stir well.

2. Cook for:
   3-4   mins for 225g (8 oz) fresh pasta
   7-10 mins for 225g (8 oz) dried pasta
   10-14 mins for 450g (1 lb) dried pasta.

   Stir occasionally during cooking, to prevent the pasta pieces sticking together. Stop cooking when the pasta is still slightly undercooked.

3. Stir well, cover and allow to stand for 5 mins before draining and serving.

PULSES – Basic method

1. Soak 225g (8 oz) pulses in plenty of cold water overnight. Alternatively, pour plenty of boiling water over the pulses, cover and allow to stand for 1-2 hours. (Split peas and lentils do not need soaking before cooking.)

2. Drain and put the pulses into a large bowl and pour over enough boiling water to cover them by at least 2.5cm (1 in).

3. Cook, stirring occasionally, until tender.
   Aduki beans: 30-35 mins
   Black-eye beans: 25-35 mins
   Cannellini beans: 30-45 mins
   Chick peas: 50-60 mins
   Flageolet beans: 35-45 mins
   Haricot beans: 25-35 mins
   Lentils: 20-30 mins
   Mung beans: 20-30 mins
   Peas: 30-45 mins
   Red kidney beans: 30-45 mins
   Split peas: 20-30 mins.

4. Cover and allow to stand for 5 mins before draining and using.

PORRIDGE
Serves 2
Cooking: 4 mins on HIGH *(100%)* *Not suitable for freezing*

50g (2 oz) porridge oats
300ml (½ pt) milk
salt, sugar, or honey

1. Put the oats in a medium bowl and add the milk. Cook, uncovered, for about 4 mins or until the porridge thickens and boils, stirring frequently.

2. Add salt, sugar or honey to taste.

MACARONI CHEESE
Serves 4
Cooking: 14 mins on HIGH *(100%) plus grilling* *Will freeze*

225g (8 oz) macaroni
40g (1½ oz) butter
40g (1½ oz) flour
2.5ml (½ tsp) mustard powder
600ml (1 pt) milk
175g (6 oz) Cheddar cheese, grated
salt and pepper

1. Put the macaroni in a large bowl and pour over enough boiling water to cover it by 2.5cm (1 in). Stir well. Cook, uncovered, for 8 mins, stirring occasionally. Allow to stand.

2. Meanwhile, put the butter, flour, mustard powder and milk into a medium bowl or jug and whisk well. Cook for about 6 mins, whisking frequently, until the sauce thickens and boils. Stir in 100g (4 oz) cheese and season to taste with salt and pepper.

3. Drain the macaroni and stir it into the sauce. Pour the mixture into a flameproof dish and sprinkle with the remaining cheese.

4. Brown under a hot grill.

VEGETABLE RISOTTO
Serves 4
Cooking: 25 mins on HIGH (100%)   Not suitable for freezing

15ml (1 tbsp) oil
25g (1 oz) butter
1 large leek, finely sliced
1 garlic clove, crushed
175g (6 oz) arborio or risotto rice
600ml (1 pt) vegetable stock
150ml (¼ pt) dry white vermouth
225g (8 oz) small broccoli florets
225g (8 oz) button mushrooms
grated Parmesan cheese, to serve

1. Put the oil, butter, leek and garlic in a large bowl, cover and cook for 5 mins.

2. Stir in the rice, cover and cook for 2 mins.

3. Add the stock and vermouth. Cook, uncovered, for 10 mins.

4. Stir in the broccoli and mushrooms and cook, uncovered, for 8 mins.

5. Cover and allow to stand for 5 mins. Serve, sprinkled with Parmesan cheese.

TURKEY PILAFF

Serves 4

Cooking: 25 mins on HIGH (100%)   Not suitable for freezing

25g (1 oz) butter
50g (2 oz) flaked almonds
10ml (2 tsp) oil
1 medium onion, finely sliced
100g (4 oz) button mushrooms
225g (8 oz) long grain rice
600ml (1 pt) boiling chicken stock
25g (1 oz) raisins
4 turkey breast fillets

1. Put the butter in a shallow heatproof dish and cook for 30 secs until melted. Add the almonds and cook for 3 mins, stirring frequently, until golden brown. Drain on kitchen paper.

2. Pour any excess butter from the almonds into a large bowl. Add the oil, onion and mushrooms, cover and cook for 3 mins.

3. Stir in the rice and cook for 3 mins.

4. Add the boiling stock and raisins. Add the turkey, pushing the pieces under the surface of the stock.

5. Cover and cook for 10 mins, stirring occasionally. Uncover and cook for a further 5 mins until the turkey is cooked through.

6. Scatter the almonds over the top to serve.

LASAGNE

Serves 4
Will freeze

Cooking: 26 mins on HIGH *(100%) and*
20 mins on MEDIUM *(50%) plus grilling*

5ml (1 tsp) oil
1 medium onion, finely chopped
1 garlic clove, crushed
350g (12 oz) lean minced beef
1 beef stock cube
15ml (1 tbsp) dried oregano
30ml (2 tbsp) tomato purée
400g can chopped tomatoes
salt and pepper
25g (1 oz) butter
25g (1 oz) plain flour
300ml (½ pt) milk
100g (4 oz) mature Cheddar cheese, grated
6 sheets no-pre-cook lasagne
25g (1 oz) Parmesan cheese, grated

1. Put the oil, onion and garlic in a large bowl, cover and cook for 5 mins, stirring once.

2. Crumble the beef and add to the bowl. Cover and cook for 5 mins, stirring twice.

3. Crumble in the beef stock cube. Add the oregano, tomato purée, tomatoes and seasoning. Cover and cook for 12 mins, stirring occasionally.

4. Put the butter, flour and milk in a bowl or jug, and whisk. Cook, uncovered, for about 4 mins, whisking frequently, until the sauce thickens and boils. Add the Cheddar cheese.

5. Grease a shallow rectangular flameproof dish. Put half the lasagne sheets in the bottom. Cover them with half the meat sauce then half the cheese sauce. Repeat these layers and scatter the Parmesan cheese over the top.

6. Cover and cook on MEDIUM (50%) for about 20 mins until the pasta is tender.

7. Brown the top of the lasagne under a hot grill.

BULGAR WHEAT SALAD

Cooking: 5 mins on HIGH *(100%)*

Serves 4–6

Not suitable for freezing

225g (8 oz) bulgar (also called burghul or cracked) wheat
600ml (1 pt) boiling vegetable stock
30ml (2 tbsp) olive oil
grated rind and juice of 1 small lemon
1 bunch spring onions, thinly sliced
half a cucumber, diced
4 tomatoes, skinned and chopped
60ml (4 tbsp) chopped fresh mint
60ml (4 tbsp) chopped fresh parsley
salt and freshly ground black pepper
10 black olives, pitted
fresh crusty bread, to serve

1. Put the bulgar wheat in a large bowl, stir in the boiling stock, cover and cook for 5 mins. Allow to stand, covered, for 15 mins.

2. Add the oil, lemon rind and juice, onions, cucumber, tomatoes, mint and parsley. Season to taste with salt and pepper. Gently stir the mixture until well mixed, then tip it into a large serving bowl.

3. Halve the olives and scatter over the salad. Serve at room temperature with crusty bread.

14

FRUIT AND DESSERTS

Fruit is perfect for cooking in the microwave, staying in shape and retaining all its juice, flavour and colour. Light sponge and suet puddings are cooked in minutes instead of taking hours of steaming on the hob. Crumbles, cheesecakes, milk puddings and egg custard are all ideal candidates for microwave cooking too, and don't forget to use the microwave to dissolve gelatine and to melt chocolate for mousses and other desserts.

Tips for cooking fruit
* Pierce or split the skins of whole fruits, such as apples, to prevent them bursting open.

* Frozen fruit can be cooked straight from the freezer.

* Add water to hard fruits and fruits with skins, such as apples and plums. 45-60ml (3-4 tbsp) is a good guide.

* Soft fruits, such as raspberries and blackcurrants; fruits with a high water content, such as rhubarb; and apple slices for a purée, usually need no additional liquid.

* Either dissolve sugar in the cooking liquid, or add sugar after cooking. Do not sprinkle sugar over fruits with skins, such as plums or blackcurrants, or the skins will toughen.

* Cover during cooking, to keep the moisture in and to help the fruit cook evenly.

* Most fruit can be cooked on HIGH (100%), but if it tends to overcook or burst open, try lowering the power to MEDIUM (50%). The difference in the cooking time will be minimal.

* Cooking times depend on the type, quantity and age of the fruit. As a guide:
    450g (1 lb) soft fruit takes 2-5 mins
    450g (1 lb) hard fruit takes 7-10 mins.

* Stir gently or reposition whole fruit occasionally during cooking.

* Allow to stand for 3-5 mins before serving.

Tips for cooking sponge and suet puddings
* When cooking a conventional recipe in the microwave, add extra liquid to the mixture. About 15ml (1 tbsp) per egg is a good guide.

* Use a pudding bowl which is large enough to allow the pudding to rise up.

* A transparent bowl allows you to see when the pudding is cooked.

* Lightly grease the bowl before adding the pudding mixture.

* Cover the pudding loosely with a 'hat' of greaseproof or non-stick paper, to keep moisture in and to allow the pudding to rise above the top of the bowl if necessary.

* Stand the bowl on a microwave rack or an upturned saucer, to encourage even cooking.

* Cook on HIGH (100%) for 3-7 mins, depending on the size of pudding.

* Stop cooking when the surface of the pudding is still slightly moist, but the mixture beneath it is cooked. The surface will dry as the pudding stands.

* Allow to stand for 3-5 mins before turning the pudding out, to let it settle.

* Turn the pudding on to a warmed plate.

* If the bottom of the pudding is still slightly undercooked, do not put it back into its bowl. Put the plated pudding back into the microwave and cook briefly until set.

Tips for cooking milk puddings
* Use a large deep bowl, to allow the pudding to boil up.

* Cook, uncovered, on HIGH (100%) until the mixture boils, then continue cooking on MEDIUM (50%) or MEDIUM-LOW (30%) until the pudding is cooked:
    semolina, tapioca and ground rice take about 10 mins
    whole rice takes 30-45 mins.

* Stir occasionally during cooking.

BAKED APPLES
Serves 4

Cooking: 5-7 mins on HIGH (100%)   Not suitable for freezing

**4 cooking apples, each weighing about 225-275g
(8-10 oz), cored
90-120ml (6-8 tbsp) mincemeat**

1. Using a small sharp knife, make a shallow cut through the skin around the middle of each apple.

2. Arrange the apples in a shallow container and add 30ml (2 tbsp) water. Cover and cook for 3 mins.

3. Fill the apple centres with mincemeat. Cover and cook for 2-4 mins until the apples are tender. Should any of the apples cook too fast and threaten to burst open, you may prefer to reduce the microwave power level to MEDIUM (50%) and continue cooking until the apples are tender.

PEARS IN CIDER
Serves 4

Cooking: 13 mins on HIGH (100%)   Not suitable for freezing

**8 small pears, peeled
300ml (½ pt) sweet cider
30ml (2 tbsp) demerara sugar
2.5ml (½ tsp) almond essence**

1. Arrange the pears, sitting them upright, around the edge of a shallow dish. Add the cider and sugar.

2. Cover and cook for about 10 mins until the pears are tender, spooning the juice over them occasionally during cooking. Carefully lift the pears on to a serving dish.

3. Return the juices to the microwave and cook, uncovered, for 2-3 mins until slightly reduced. Add the almond essence and serve the sauce with the pears. Serve hot or chilled.

HONEY-BAKED BANANAS

Serves 4

Cooking: 6 mins on HIGH (100%)   *Not suitable for freezing*

25g (1 oz) butter
juice of 1 medium orange
15ml (1 tbsp) clear honey
4 medium bananas
whipped cream or ice cream to serve

1. Put the butter, orange juice and honey in a shallow dish. Cook for 2 mins until the butter has melted. Stir well.

2. Skin the bananas and halve them lengthways. Add to the dish, turning to coat them well with the butter mixture.

3. Cook for 3-4 mins until the bananas just begin to bubble. Serve with whipped cream or ice cream.

APPLE AND BLACKBERRY CRUMBLE   *Serves 4*

Cooking: 10 mins on HIGH (100%)   *Not suitable for freezing*

450g (1 lb) cooking apples, peeled, cored and sliced
30ml (2 tbsp) sugar
225g (8 oz) fresh or frozen blackberries
75g (3 oz) block (hard) margarine
175g (6 oz) plain flour
75g (3 oz) demerara sugar

1. Put the apples and sugar in a 20.5cm (8 in) soufflé dish with 15ml (1 tbsp) water. Cover and cook for 3 mins. Stir in the blackberries.

2. Rub the margarine into the flour until the mixture resembles fine breadcrumbs. Stir in the sugar. Tip the mixture on top of the fruit and level the surface.

3. Cook, uncovered, for about 7 mins. Allow to stand for a few mins before serving.

RICE PUDDING   *Serves 4*
Cooking: 7 mins on HIGH (100%) and
*   30-45 mins on MEDIUM-LOW (30%) plus*
*   grilling, if wished*
Not suitable for freezing

50g (2 oz) pudding rice
600ml (1 pt) milk
25g (1 oz) sugar
ground nutmeg
15g (½ oz) butter

1. Put the rice, milk and sugar into a large bowl. Sprinkle with nutmeg and add the butter.

2. Cook for about 7 mins, stirring twice, or until boiling. Cover and cook on MEDIUM-LOW (30%) for 30-45 mins, stirring occasionally, until thick and creamy.

3. If wished, pour the pudding into a flameproof dish and brown lightly under a hot grill.

EGG CUSTARD   *Serves 4*
Cooking: 15-20 mins on MEDIUM (50%)
Not suitable for freezing

3 eggs
600ml (1 pt) milk
25g (1 oz) caster sugar
ground nutmeg

1. Lightly beat the eggs, then gradually beat in the milk. Strain the mixture into a dish, then stir in the sugar and sprinkle with nutmeg.

2. Stand the dish in a larger container with sufficient boiling water to come half way up the dish.

3. Cook, uncovered, on MEDIUM (50%) for 15-20 mins until just set. Allow to stand for 5 mins before serving.

APRICOT UPSIDE DOWN PUDDING

Serves 6
Will freeze

Cooking: 11 mins on HIGH (100%)

411g can apricot halves in fruit juice
25g (1 oz) butter
25g (1 oz) soft brown sugar
150g (5 oz) soft margarine
150g (5 oz) caster sugar
2 eggs, beaten
175g (6 oz) self-raising flour, sieved

1. Drain the apricots, reserving 75ml (5 tbsp) of the juice.

2. Put the butter in a 20.5cm (8 in) soufflé dish and cook for 45 secs or until melted. Brush the base and sides of the dish with the butter, then scatter the brown sugar on to the buttered surface. Arrange the apricots, cut side upwards, in the base of the dish.

3. Cream the margarine and caster sugar together until light and fluffy. Add the eggs, a little at a time, beating well after each addition. Fold in the flour and the reserved fruit juice.

4. Spread the pudding mixture over the apricots and level the surface.

5. Place the dish on a microwave rack or upturned saucer and cook, uncovered, for about 10 mins until the surface is still slightly moist but the pudding beneath it is cooked.

6. Allow to stand for 5 mins before turning out on to a warmed plate.

SYRUP SPONGE PUDDING

Cooking: 6 mins on HIGH *(100%)*

Serves 4

Will freeze

30ml (2 tbsp) golden syrup
50g (2 oz) margarine
50g (2 oz) caster sugar
1 egg, beaten
100g (4 oz) self-raising flour
few drops of vanilla essence
45ml (3 tbsp) milk

1. Butter a 600ml (1 pt) pudding basin and put the syrup in the bottom.

2. Put the margarine, sugar, egg, flour and vanilla essence in a bowl and beat well until smooth. Gradually stir in the milk. Spoon the mixture on top of the syrup and level the surface.

3. Cover loosely with a 'hat' of greaseproof paper and place the pudding on a microwave rack or upturned saucer. Cook for about 6 mins until the surface is still slightly moist but the pudding beneath it is cooked. Allow to stand for 5 mins before turning out on to a warmed plate.

BLACKCURRANT CHEESECAKE

Serves 6

Cooking: 1 min on HIGH (100%) and   *Will freeze*
8 mins on MEDIUM (50%) plus cooling

You need a blender or processor for this recipe.

50g (2 oz) butter
100g (4 oz) digestive biscuits, crushed
175g (6 oz) soft cream cheese
100g (4 oz) cottage cheese
2 eggs, beaten
30ml (2 tbsp) caster sugar
5ml (1 tsp) cornflour
397g can blackcurrant pie filling

1. Lightly grease an 18cm (7 in) flan dish.

2. Put the butter in a bowl and cook for 1 min until melted.
   Add the biscuits and stir well. Press the mixture into the
   base of the flan dish.

3. Put the cream cheese, cottage cheese, eggs, sugar and
   cornflour into a blender or processor and purée until
   smooth. Pour on to the biscuit base.

4. Cook, uncovered, on MEDIUM (50%) for about 8 mins or
   until set (don't worry if the centre is still slightly moist —
   this will set as the cheesecake cools).

5. Allow to cool before spreading the pie filling over the top
   of the cheesecake.

WHITE CHOCOLATE MOUSSE

Serves 4-6

Cooking: 4 mins on MEDIUM-LOW (30%) and
45 secs on HIGH (100%)

Will freeze

175g (6 oz) white chocolate
15ml (1 tbsp) clear honey
5ml (1 tsp) gelatine
150ml (¼ pt) whipping cream
2 egg whites
pinch salt
25g (1 oz) white or plain chocolate, to decorate

1. Break the white chocolate into a bowl. Add 45ml (3 tbsp) water and the honey. Cook on MEDIUM-LOW (30%) for about 4 mins. Stir well until melted and smooth.

2. Put 45ml (3 tbsp) water in a small bowl and sprinkle the gelatine over. Allow it to stand for 1 min. Cook on HIGH (100%) for 30-45 secs, stirring every 15 secs, until clear (make sure it does not boil). Stir into the white chocolate.

3. Whip the cream until it stands in soft peaks. Fold it into the chocolate mixture.

4. Using a clean bowl and whisk, whisk the egg whites with the salt until stiff. Fold into the chocolate mixture. Spoon into 4-6 small glasses and chill until set.

5. To decorate, chill the remaining chocolate, then make chocolate shavings by drawing a potato peeler across it. Sprinkle some on to the top of each mousse.

CHOCOLATE MOUSSE   *Serves 4*
Cooking: 4 mins on MEDIUM (50%) plus chilling
Will freeze

225g (8 oz) plain chocolate
40g (1½ oz) butter
4 eggs, separated
20ml (4 tsp) rum
whipped cream and grated chocolate, to decorate

1. Break the chocolate into a bowl and add the butter. Cook on
   MEDIUM (50%) for about 4 mins, stirring occasionally, until
   melted.

2. Beat in the egg yolks and rum. Whisk the egg whites until
   stiff and fold them into the chocolate mixture.

3. Spoon into 4 serving dishes or glasses and chill for about
   2 hours until set. Decorate with whipped cream and grated
   chocolate to serve.

APPLE AND SPICE CAKE – see page 139

15

CAKES, BISCUITS
AND SWEETS

Cakes cooked in the microwave rise well and their flavour is good. Their texture is slightly pudding-like and they do not brown and crisp (though a combination oven, which browns as well as microwaves, will bake some cakes successfully). Generally, very moist mixtures are suited to microwave cooking, as are recipes in which the fats and sugars are melted together. The microwave recipes in this section have been tried and tested over the years.

Some biscuit recipes can be microwaved but because they can only be cooked in small batches, and need frequent attention, it is more convenient to cook them conventionally. However, shortbread and flapjacks are successful and I have included the recipes for these, together with microwave meringues.

Lastly, the microwave makes speedy work of melting butter, chocolate, and so on, for sweets − a few recipes are included.

Tips for making cakes

* Choose circular dishes with vertical sides. Ring moulds produce the most successful cakes, with no chance of the centre remaining uncooked.

* When trying a recipe for the first time, choose a deep container − cakes rise considerably during cooking. Half fill it only.

* Lightly grease the cooking container. Do not coat it with flour or a disagreeable crust will form on the outside of the cake.

* Line the base of the container with non-stick baking paper or greased greaseproof paper, for easy removal of the cake.

* When cooking a conventional recipe in the microwave, add extra liquid to the mixture − about 15ml (1 tbsp) per egg is a good guide. Fruit cakes should have a very soft dropping consistency (see page 138).

* Plump up dried fruit before adding it to a cake mixture (see method on page 138).

* Sugar must be well blended into the mixture − lumps of sugar attract microwaves and burn easily.

* Small cakes should be arranged in a circle in the microwave, with the centre left free.

* Place the dish on a microwave rack to make sure the cake cooks evenly.

* Cook sponge-type cakes on HIGH (100%) and fruit cakes on MEDIUM (50%) or MEDIUM-LOW (30%). Check with your oven manufacturer's instruction book too.

* Stop cooking when the surface of the cake is still slightly moist but the mixture beneath it is cooked. The surface will dry out as it stands.

* Allow a standing time before turning the cake out − 5 mins for sponge-type cakes and 20 mins for fruit cakes.

* Turn the cake out on to a cooling rack lined with non-stick baking paper − to prevent it sticking to the rack.

CHOCOLATE CAKE
Cooking: 6-7 mins on HIGH *(100%)*

Serves 6-8
Will freeze

200g (7 oz) self-raising flour
5ml (1 tsp) baking powder
2.5ml (½ tsp) bicarbonate of soda
30ml (2 tbsp) cocoa powder
75g (3 oz) caster sugar
2 eggs, beaten
150ml (¼ pt) corn or sunflower oil
150ml (¼ pt) milk
30ml (2 tbsp) golden syrup

1. Grease a 20.5cm (8 in) cake or soufflé dish and line its base with a circle of non-stick baking paper.

2. Sieve the flour, baking powder, bicarbonate of soda and cocoa into a medium bowl. Stir in the sugar.

3. Whisk together the eggs, oil, milk and syrup. Add to the dry ingredients and beat well until smooth. Pour the mixture into the prepared dish.

4. Place the dish on a microwave rack or upturned saucer. Cook for 6-7 mins until the surface is still slightly moist but the cake beneath it is cooked. Allow to stand for 10 mins before turning the cake out on to a cooling rack lined with non-stick baking paper.

LEMON SPONGE RING
Cooking: 7 mins on HIGH *(100%)*

Serves 8
Will freeze

150g (5 oz) caster sugar, plus extra for coating
175g (6 oz) self-raising flour
5ml (1 tsp) baking powder
175g (6 oz) soft margarine
3 eggs, beaten
30ml (2 tbsp) lemon curd
Topping:
60ml (4 tbsp) lemon juice
45ml (3 tbsp) caster sugar
crystallised lemon slices

1. Grease a medium ring mould and lightly coat the greased surface with the extra caster sugar.

2. Sieve the flour with the baking powder.

3. Cream the margarine and 150g (5 oz) caster sugar together until light and fluffy. Add the eggs, a little at a time, beating well after each addition. Fold in the flour mixture.

4. Put the lemon curd into a small bowl and cook for 45 secs until melted. Stir into the cake mixture with 30ml (2 tbsp) warm water. Pour into the prepared ring mould.

5. Cook for about 6 mins until the surface is still slightly moist but the cake beneath it is cooked. Allow to stand for 2-3 mins before turning the cake out on to a cooling rack lined with non-stick baking paper.

6. To make the topping, mix the lemon juice with the caster sugar and pour over the warm cake. Decorate with lemon slices and allow to cool.

FRUIT CAKE RING

Serves 16

Cooking: 5 mins on HIGH (100%) and
*   50 mins on MEDIUM-LOW (30%)*

Will freeze

500g (1 lb 2 oz) mixed dried fruit
150ml (¼ pt) orange or apple juice
250g (9 oz) plain flour
5ml (1 tsp) mixed spice
5ml (1 tsp) ground ginger
5ml (1 tsp) ground nutmeg
175g (6 oz) butter, softened
175g (6 oz) soft dark brown sugar
4 eggs
30ml (2 tbsp) black treacle
50g (2 oz) walnuts, chopped
100g (4 oz) glacé cherries, chopped
45ml (3 tbsp) milk

1. Grease a 2 litre (3½ pt) ring mould and line its base with non-stick baking paper.

2. Put the fruit and orange or apple juice in a bowl, cover and cook for 5 mins until plumped up and soft.

3. Sieve the flour with the spice, ginger and nutmeg. Cream the butter and sugar together until light and fluffy. Add the eggs, one at a time, adding 15ml (1 tbsp) flour with each one. Add the remaining ingredients and stir in the warm fruit and juice to make a very soft dropping consistency.

4. Pour the mixture into the prepared mould and level the surface.

5. Cook, uncovered, on MEDIUM-LOW (30%) for 45-50 mins until a wooden cocktail stick, inserted in the cake, comes out clean.

6. Allow to stand for 20 mins, then turn out on to a cooling rack lined with non-stick baking paper. Strip off the paper and allow the cake to cool (any moisture on the surface will dry as it cools).

APPLE AND SPICE CAKE

Serves 16

Cooking: 9-10 mins on HIGH *(100%)*   *Will freeze*

450g (1 lb) eating apples, peeled, cored and finely chopped
100g (4 oz) plain white flour
100g (4 oz) plain wholemeal flour
10ml (2 tsp) baking powder
7.5ml (1½ tsp) mixed spice
175g (6 oz) soft brown sugar
100g (4 oz) soft margarine
2 eggs
90ml (6 tbsp) milk
sifted icing sugar, to serve

1. Grease a 1.7 litre (3 pt) ring mould and line the base with non-stick baking paper. Arrange one-third of the apple on top of the paper.

2. Put the white and wholemeal flours, baking powder, spice, sugar, margarine, eggs and milk into a large bowl and beat until smooth.

3. Fold in the remaining apple.

4. Spoon the mixture into the ring mould and level the top.

5. Cook, uncovered, for 9-10 mins until the surface is still slightly moist but the cake beneath it is cooked. Allow to stand for 15 mins, then turn the cake out onto a plate. Dust with icing sugar to serve. Delicious served warm.

ALMOND SLICES

Cooking: 4 mins on HIGH *(100%)*

Makes 6
Will freeze

100g (4 oz) soft margarine
75g (3 oz) clear honey
1 egg, beaten
75g (3 oz) plain flour, sifted
75g (3 oz) ground almonds
25g (1 oz) flaked almonds, toasted
sifted icing sugar, to serve

1. Lightly grease a 20.5cm (8 in) flan dish and line the base with non-stick paper.

2. Cream the margarine and honey until light and fluffy. Beat in the egg, then fold in the flour and ground almonds.

3. Tip the mixture into the prepared dish and level the top. Sprinkle the flaked almonds over the top. Place the dish on a microwave rack or upturned saucer and cook, uncovered, for about 4 mins until firm.

4. Allow to stand for 5 mins in the dish, then turn out onto a cooling rack. Allow to cool completely before cutting into wedges.

5. Dust with icing sugar to serve.

CORNFLAKE CRISPIES
Makes 12
Cooking: 4-5 mins on MEDIUM *(50%) Not suitable for freezing*

225g (8 oz) plain chocolate
50g (2 oz) butter
15ml (1 tbsp) golden syrup
50g (2 oz) cornflakes

1. Break the chocolate into a medium bowl and add the butter and syrup. Cook on MEDIUM (50%) for 4-5 mins, stirring frequently, until melted.

2. Fold in the cornflakes.

3. Put spoonfuls into paper cake cases and chill until set.

MICROWAVE MERINGUES
Makes about 24
Cooking: 4½-6 mins on HIGH *(100%) Not suitable for freezing*

1 egg white
275-350g (10-12 oz) icing sugar
whipped cream, to serve

1. Lightly whisk the egg white to break it up. Sieve the icing sugar to remove all lumps. Line the microwave turntable, or a large heatproof plate, with non-stick baking paper.

2. Beat the icing sugar into the egg white, a little at a time, until you have a firm fondant-like paste.

3. Divide the mixture into small balls and arrange eight at a time, in a circle, on the baking paper. Cook, uncovered, for 1½-2 mins until risen and firm to the touch (take care not to overcook them).

4. Allow them to cool before carefully lifting them off the paper. Serve with whipped cream.

SHORTBREAD

Makes 6-8 wedges

Cooking: 4 mins on HIGH (100%) *Will freeze*

110g (4 oz) butter, softened
50g (2 oz) caster sugar, plus extra for sprinkling
150g (5 oz) plain flour
25g (1 oz) semolina

1. Grease an 18cm (7 in) flan dish or plate and line the base with non-stick baking paper.

2. Cream the butter and sugar together until light and fluffy.

3. Sieve the flour and semolina. Fold them into the mixture, then lightly knead it to form a dough.

4. Press the dough into the dish or plate and level the surface. Prick well with a fork. Cook for 4 mins or until set.

5. Allow to stand for 5 mins then mark into wedges and sprinkle with extra caster sugar. Cool completely before lifting them off the paper.

CHOCOLATE BISCUIT BISCUITS   *Makes 10*
Cooking: 3 mins on MEDIUM *(50%) Not suitable for freezing*

100g (4 oz) plain chocolate
100g (4 oz) butter
15ml (1 tbsp) clear honey
30ml (2 tbsp) double cream
100g (4 oz) digestive biscuits, crumbled
50g (2 oz) chopped nuts
25g (1 oz) no-soak dried apricots, finely chopped
25g (1 oz) glacé cherries, chopped

1. Lightly grease a 20.5cm (8 in) flan dish and line the base with non-stick baking paper.

2. Break the chocolate into a large bowl. Cut the butter into cubes and add to the chocolate with the honey. Cook on MEDIUM (50%) for about 3 mins, stirring frequently, until melted.

3. Stir in the remaining ingredients.

4. Tip the mixture into the prepared dish and level the top. Chill until just set, mark into 10 wedges, then chill until firm.

FLAPJACKS

Makes 16

Cooking: 4-5 mins on HIGH *(100%)*
Will freeze

75g (3 oz) butter
50g (2 oz) soft brown sugar
30ml (2 tbsp) golden syrup
175g (6 oz) porridge oats

1. Grease a shallow 12.5 × 23cm (5 × 9 in) dish.

2. Put the butter, sugar and syrup in a bowl and cook for 2 mins, stirring once, until the sugar has dissolved. Stir well, then add the oats. Stir well again.

3. Tip the mixture into the dish and press it in well. Stand the dish on a microwave rack or upturned saucer and cook for 2-3 mins until firm to touch.

4. Allow to cool slightly before marking into 16 pieces. Cool completely before turning out of the dish.

WHITE CHOCOLATE CLUSTERS *Makes 12 sweets*

Cooking: 3-4 mins on HIGH *(100%) and*
4 mins on MEDIUM-LOW *(30%)*
Not suitable for freezing

40g (1½ oz) flaked almonds
75g (3 oz) white chocolate
25g (1 oz) crystallised ginger, finely chopped
25g (1 oz) no-soak dried apricots, finely chopped

1. Put the almonds in a shallow heatproof dish and cook for 3-4 mins, stirring frequently, until lightly browned.

2. Break the chocolate into a bowl and cook on MEDIUM-LOW (30%) for about 4 mins, stirring occasionally, until melted. Stir in the almonds, ginger and apricots.

3. Put small spoonfuls of the mixture into paper sweet cases and chill until firm.

ALMOND AND COCONUT FUDGE

Cooking: 1 min on HIGH (100%)   *Makes 16 slices*
            plus chilling   *Will freeze*

50g (2 oz) plain chocolate
50g (2 oz) unsalted butter
50g (2 oz) dark brown sugar
15ml (1 tbsp) milk
25g (1 oz) ground almonds
50g (2 oz) macaroons, crushed
25g (1 oz) desiccated coconut
icing sugar

1. Break the chocolate into a bowl and add the butter, sugar and milk. Cook for about 1 min, stirring once or twice, until melted.

2. Stir in the almonds, macaroons and coconut. Cover and refrigerate for about 30 mins or until the mixture is firm enough to handle.

3. Tip the mixture on to a sheet of non-stick baking paper or greaseproof paper and shape it into a sausage about 23cm (9 in) long. Wrap it well, twisting the ends like a Christmas cracker. Chill for 1 hour or more.

4. Remove the paper, sieve some icing sugar over the fudge and cut it into 1cm (½ in) slices.

MUESLI BITES

Makes about 28

Cooking: 3 mins on MEDIUM *(50%)*   *Not suitable for freezing*

100g (4 oz) plain chocolate
50g (2 oz) butter
50g (2 oz) golden syrup
225g (8 oz) breakfast muesli

1. Break the chocolate into a bowl and add the butter and syrup. Cook on MEDIUM (50%) for about 3 mins, stirring frequently, until melted.

2. Stir in the muesli.

3. Put small spoonfuls of the mixture into paper sweet cases and allow to cool until set.

CHOCOLATE TRUFFLES
Cooking: 2-3 mins on MEDIUM *(50%)*
plus 30 mins cooling and firming time

Makes about 24
Will freeze

100g (4 oz) plain chocolate
50g (2 oz) butter
100g (4 oz) trifle sponges
25g (1 oz) icing sugar
15ml (1 tbsp) brandy or rum
cocoa powder, icing sugar or chocolate vermicelli

1. Break the chocolate into a bowl and add the butter. Cook on
   MEDIUM (50%) for 2-3 mins, stirring frequently, until melted.

2. Finely crumble the sponges and sieve the sugar. Stir the
   sponge crumbs, sugar and brandy or rum into the chocolate.

3. Allow to cool for about 30 mins until firm enough to handle.
   Shape into small balls and coat them with sifted cocoa powder
   or icing sugar or chocolate vermicelli. Refrigerate until firm.

16

... AND DON'T FORGET

Baby foods and drinks

Microwaving is a quick, convenient and hygienic way of heating baby food. Take care not to overheat it and be sure to stir frequently during heating. Always test it yourself, before giving it to baby, to check it is not too hot.

Baby milk should be heated with care. Remember, the bottle can feel cool to the touch while pockets of the milk inside it are extremely hot. Shake the bottle well before putting it in the microwave. 100ml (4 fl oz) takes 20-30 secs on HIGH (100%), 225ml (8 fl oz) takes 40-50 secs. Shake again after heating and check the temperature carefully before giving it to baby.

Bread

Warm fresh bread or freshen up stale bread in your microwave. Whole loaves, rolls or slices should be heated on MEDIUM (50%) or MEDIUM-LOW (30%) until warmed through.

Combination ovens cook bread beautifully and you should find instructions in your manufacturer's instruction book. You can find recipes for Soda Bread and two delicious flavoured breads in *The Combination Microwave Cook* written with my friend and colleague Caroline Young.

Butter

Soften butter for spreading or baking. 100g (4 oz) takes about 30 secs on MEDIUM-LOW (30%).

Chocolate

To melt chocolate, break it into a bowl and cook on MEDIUM (50%) or MEDIUM-LOW (30%), stirring frequently, until melted. Do not overheat it.

Drinks

The microwave is ideal for heating individual drinks, so long as these basic rules are followed:

* Use a large cup or mug with sloping sides (that is, the top is wider than the bottom).

* Stir the drink before putting it into the microwave and occasionally during heating.

* Do not heat milk in its milk bottle.

Gelatine

To dissolve gelatine, choose one of the following methods:

1. Sprinkle it on to water, or some of the liquid from the recipe, and allow to stand for 1 min. Heat, stirring every 30 secs, until the gelatine has dissolved. Do not boil.

2. Heat some of the liquid from the ingredients until it is very hot, but not quite boiling. Quickly add the gelatine, stirring briskly until dissolved.

Herbs

Many fresh herbs can be dried in the microwave. Small-leaf or chopped herbs work best. Chopped chives, mint and sage are suitable; leaves of thyme and rosemary are good too. Basil is not so successful because it burns easily and loses its flavour (it is best frozen). Parsley also tends to lose its flavour.

Arrange the washed and dried leaves (or chopped herbs) in a shallow even layer on kitchen paper (not recycled paper – it may burn). Heat on MEDIUM, stirring or repositioning frequently and checking every 30 secs or so, until the herbs are dry and will crumble when rubbed between your fingers. Allow to stand for 10 mins before storing in airtight containers.

Jam
Melt jam to spread on cakes. Heat it carefully or it will become too hot.

Jelly
Save time by melting jelly cubes in the microwave. Break the jelly into a bowl or jug and add 150ml (¼ pt) water. Cook for 2 mins until melted. Stir well and top up the jelly with cold water.

Oranges and lemons
Squeeze extra juice from oranges and lemons after warming them in the microwave first. Heat them for 1-2 mins.

Preserves
Small batches of jams, jellies, marmalades and chutneys are very succesful in the microwave. You will find guidelines and recipes in 'The Microwave Planner'.

INDEX

THE CURRY SECRET

This is the curry book with a difference! It gives the secret of *Indian restaurant cooking* – that particularly interesting and distinctive variety that is served in Indian restaurants all over the world. Kris Dhillon writes with the authority of an accomplished Indian restaurateur, with many years of experience and thousands of satisfied customers. Most chefs guard the secret of their basic curry sauce closely but here Kris Dhillon reveals all, and offers you the opportunity to reproduce that elusive taste in your own kitchen.

CHINESE COOKERY SECRETS
How To Cook Chinese Restaurant Food At Home

Best-selling author and cookery consultant Deh-Ta Hsiung shares his life-long knowledge of Chinese *restaurant* cooking to help you reproduce your favourite meals at home – from a simple single dish to an elaborate, grand feast. In a clear, straightforward style, he vividly reveals the elusive secrets that produce perfection. He shows each crucial stage of preparation to enable you to recreate the harmonious blending of subtle flavours, delicate textures, aromas, colours and shapes that are the hallmarks of authentic Chinese *restaurant* cooking.

Uniform with this book

FOOD PROCESSORS
PROPERLY EXPLAINED

With a food processor in your kitchen a whole new range of mouthwatering possibilities opens up. Not just pâtés and terrines, but different ideas for soups, vegetables, meats, pastries and cakes. Discover for yourself that there is far more to a food processor than just slicing, chopping, shredding and liquidising. Includes over 160 recipes created by the author and approved by family and friends.

SLOW COOKING
PROPERLY EXPLAINED

Electric slow cookers offer many advantages. The food tastes better and doesn't burn or boil over. Tough cuts of meat become more tender, and you can cook delicious soups, stews and casseroles. *And* you save a lot of electricity. Designed for those who are buying (or thinking of buying) their first slow cooker, as well as for the more experienced user, this book has become *the* standard work on the subject. Full of useful information and ideas, it contains over 100 recipes for tasty and nourishing dishes.

Uniform with this book

RIGHT WAY
PUBLISHING POLICY

HOW WE SELECT TITLES

RIGHT WAY consider carefully every deserving manuscript. Where an author is an authority on his subject but an inexperienced writer, we provide first-class editorial help. The standards we set make sure that every **RIGHT WAY** book is practical, easy to understand, concise, informative and delightful to read. Our specialist artists are skilled at creating simple illustrations which augment the text wherever necessary.

CONSISTENT QUALITY

At every reprint our books are updated where appropriate, giving our authors the opportunity to include new information.

FAST DELIVERY

We sell **RIGHT WAY** books to the best bookshops throughout the world. It may be that your bookseller has run out of stock of a particular title. If so, he can order more from us at any time – we have a fine reputation for ''same day'' despatch, and we supply any order, however small (even a single copy), to any bookseller who has an account with us. We prefer you to buy from your bookseller, as this reminds him of the strong underlying public demand for **RIGHT WAY** books. However, you can order direct from us by post or by phone with a credit card.

FREE

If you would like an up-to-date list of all **RIGHT WAY** titles currently available, please send a stamped self-addressed envelope to ELLIOT RIGHT WAY BOOKS, BRIGHTON ROAD, LOWER KINGSWOOD, TADWORTH, SURREY, KT20 6TD, U.K. or visit our web site at www.right-way.co.uk